CW00516551

How to Trade Options

The Complete Guide for Beginners

2nd Edition

By Tim Morris

ISBN: 9798850563233
Published by ZML Corp LLC

Table of Contents

This Page Intentionally Left Blank

Disclaimer

This book is for entertainment and informational purposes only. Investing in the stock market involves a great deal of risk, and past performance is not a guarantee of future results. You are responsible for your own behavior and none of this book should be considered legal, personal, or financial advice. Neither the author nor publisher is a licensed broker or investment advisor. Talk to a licensed financial advisor before making any investment decisions. It is illegal to copy or distribute any part of this book without written consent from the author or publisher. Copyright © 2023, all rights reserved. Written by Tim Morris. Published by ZML Corp LLC.

About the Author

Hi, my name is Tim Morris. I have been trading stocks and options for many years and have written a number of books related to investing.

What you'll come to find is — and something you may already know — there are a lot of *charlatans* in the stock "educator" world. Anyone can write a book and anyone can claim to be an expert in a subject. But just because they use big words and include intriguing imagery doesn't mean their strategies actually work or that they hold any true insight in the field.

When I publish a book, I stand by what I write. Wild claims and "get rich quick" schemes draw readers attention, but they don't survive the test of time. I want readers to do *well* in the markets with the advice that I provide. This in turn earns readers trust, proving that I am a knowledgeable figure in the field. In addition, I keep an up-to-date track record on my website — an almost non-existent find in the stock educator world.

I also make sure to consistently stay on top of market analysis, editing and revising my books in the process. There's even been circumstances where I have spent considerable time, money, and effort to create a book, only to take it off the shelf because it hasn't performed up to the standards I want to keep as an author.

Finance is an important part of life. My ultimate goal as an author is to help you get past the inordinate amount of junk you may find on the internet and teach you investment strategies that will actually make you financially successful.

If you'd like know more about me, learn tips related to profiting in the stock market, as well as view other books I've written that are not available on Amazon, you can go to my website at TradeMoreStocks.com.

Introduction

In this book, we will be going over the wonderful world of options. I'm going to assume you have some knowledge of the stock market, but are new to the options world. While aspects between the two are related, there are many distinct differences that only pertain to options trading.

If you're reading this book, you're curious about what the option market has to offer. I must admit, when I first started trading stocks, I wasn't very good. I would buy high and sell low, losing quite a bit of money in the process. I think most people can relate to this, as it takes time to become good at anything, and the stock market is no exception.

As I continued to study and learn, I started having more success in the markets. Being naturally intrigued, one day I decided to branch out and learn about options. At first I thought they were silly. A contract... why wouldn't you just buy the stock?

However, as I furthered my studies into options, I started to appreciate them more and more. Compared to stocks, there were a lot more choices than just "buy" or "sell." I could short a stock using a put option without paying "interest fees." If a stock stayed flat, there were methods which allowed me to profit from the lack of movement. There were even strategies where I could combine multiple options together to limit risk and capital on a trade.

Long story short, I now invest using both stocks and options. They each have their strengths and weaknesses, and can be combined to better diversify an investor's portfolio.

This book is laid out into five chapters. In *Chapter 1* we will be going over the fundamentals of options and the reasons behind trading them. In *Chapter 2*, we will start using this information to partake in basic option strategies. In *Chapters 3 and 4*, we'll continue expanding on our knowledge to learn more advanced option strategies. Then, in *Chapter 5*, we'll go over what I consider to be the best option strategies to implement in your own portfolio (and why).

I must mention, there is a stark contrast to what textbooks reveal compared to what occurs in real world options trading. Considering this, as I teach you subject matter in this book, I will also provide my professional opinion.

Having me as your mentor, someone who can guide you through the process, can save you a lot time and costly mistakes when you're learning a new subject like this. So without further ado, let's get started learning about options!

Chapter 1
What is an Option

In the United States, options are handled by the Chicago Board Options Exchange (CBOE). This means the CBOE is where your orders are processed when you buy or sell options. At first glance, options may be rather confusing. I remember it took me a while to wrap my head around them considering they are so different from stocks.

With a stock, you are buying part ownership in a company — a tangible quality. You know what a company is, you understand you own a part of it, etc. Well... options are different. You're not buying any part of a company, but instead establishing a contract in the open market with another individual which just *correlates* to a company. Put another way, an option is just an agreement between two people. It really has no affiliation with a company, except for the fact it relates to a company's stock price.

These agreements have time limits on them, which are known as *expiration dates*. Depending at what price the underlying stock closes upon expiration determines if the option expires "worthless" (*out of the money*), or if the agreement is assigned to the option buyer (*in the money*).

There are two types of options: a **call** option and a **put** option. With both, you can either be the *buyer* or the *seller*. We will touch briefly on buying and selling options in this chapter, diving into more detailed examples later on in the book.

Buying Options

When you *buy* an option, you are entering into an agreement with the option seller. This agreement states 100 shares of stock will be provided to you at a specified price (*strike price*) on a specified date (*expiration date*) for each option contract purchased.

When you buy a **call** option, you want the price of the stock to *increase* in value. While not dollar a dollar match, call options move in tandem with the underlying stock price (USP). Put another way, as the stock price increases, so does the price of the call option.

When you buy a **put** option, you want the underlying stock price to *decrease* in value. Similar to "shorting," you make money with put options as the underlying stock price (USP) decreases in value. And just like a call option, puts are purchased from an option seller.

Selling Options

As the option *seller*, you are entering into an agreement with the option buyer. This agreement states you will provide 100 shares of stock for a specified price (*strike price*) at a specified time (*expiration date*) for each option contract sold.

When you sell a call option, you collect a lump sum (*e.g. $30*) which is called the *premium*. Your ultimate goal as a call option seller is for the USP to expire *below* the strike price of the option you sold. When this occurs, the option expires "worthless," allowing you keep the premium from the sale without having to provide the buyer any shares of stock.

When you *sell* a **put** option, you again collect a lump sum. However, as a put option *seller*, your ultimate goal is for the USP to expire *above* the strike price of the option you sold. So long as the USP stays above the strike price by expiration, you collect your full premium and the option expires "worthless."

◆ ◆ ◆

Because of the fact there is less much volume in the options market (compared to the stock market), not all stocks allow you to trade options. There has to be enough interest surrounding a company in order for the CBOE to allow options to be associated with it. This is why many larger companies have options, while some newer, smaller companies do not.

Of the stocks that do allow options trading all have, at the very least, *monthly* options. This is where their options expire on the third Friday of the month.

Some more heavily traded stocks and ETFs have long-term equity anticipation (LEAP) options, weekly options, or even tri-weekly options (*e.g. expire Monday, Wednesday, Friday*). Again, this all relates to the amount of interest and volume surrounding a company or ETF, in regards to if the CBOE allow these types of options.

I will be showing pictures throughout the book from the popular broker known as Robinhood. A beneficial aspect of this broker, compared to others, is they offer commission-free trading for both stocks *and* options. While most brokers have transitioned to commission free stock trading, many still charge fees to trade options.

Using a broker like Robinhood, especially if you have a small account, can save you quite a bit in trading commissions (if you don't currently use Robinhood, you can use the following link and you'll receive a free stock worth up to $200 just for signing up: linkpony.com/robinhood).

Options Chain

When you search for a stock symbol with your broker, you will see something known as the "options chain." This is a list that shows you the premiums of call and put options at different *strike prices* and *expiration dates* (two terms which are important to remember). I have an example labeled numerically below with the company Snapchat (SNAP).

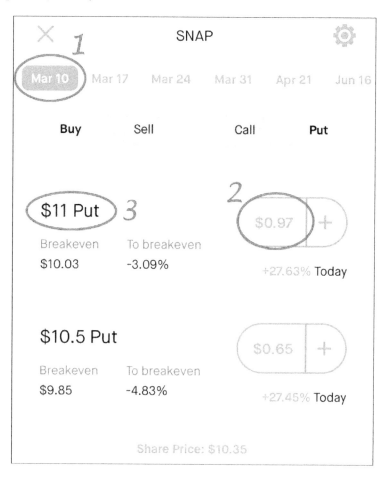

In the picture on the previous page, which displays a put option chain for the stock SNAP, you will notice three things labeled:

1) Expiration Date
2) Option Price (*premium*)
3) Strike Price

The **expiration date** is the date when the option expires. On this date, the value of the *underlying stock price* (USP) at the end of the trading day determines whether an option is in-the-money (*assigned*) or out-of-the-money (*worthless*). Options technically expire at 11:59pm on the date of expiration, but the latest that public holders can exercise their options contracts is 5:30pm.

The option price is what you pay when you buy an option or what you receive when you sell an option; it is also known as the option **premium**.

The **strike price** is the price you choose when buying or selling an option in which the underlying security (*stock*) can be exercised. This can be further defined by the following terms:

▶ **In the Money** (ITM) – When you buy an ITM **call** option, the strike price is currently *below* the USP. When you buy an ITM **put** option, the strike price is currently *above* the USP.

▷ *Stock XYZ trades for $50. A **call** option with a strike price of $48 would be considered ITM. A **put** option with a strike price of $52 would be considered ITM.*

▶ **At the Money** (ATM) – An ATM option is the closest strike price available to the USP at that given time.

▷ *Stock XYZ is trading for $50.20. A call or put option with a strike price of $50 would both be considered ATM.*

▶ **Out of the Money** (OTM) – When you buy an OTM **call** option, the strike price is currently *above* the USP. When you buy an OTM **put** option, the strike price is currently *below* the USP.

> ▷ *Stock XYZ is trading for $50. A* **call** *option with a strike price of $55 would be considered OTM. A* **put** *option with a strike price of $45 would be considered OTM.*

Options can only expire OTM or ITM. This relates to whether the option is assigned or is deemed worthless upon expiration.

Something else to note is every option contract corresponds with 100 shares of stock, which will be better understood as we go over examples throughout the book.

ITM Expiration Example

Stock XYZ is currently trading for **$52**. An **ITM** call option with a strike price of $50, and an expiration date one week away, trades for $2.50. To rephrase, this option has a *premium* of $2.50.

Because one option corresponds to 100 shares of stock, all option prices shown must be multiplied by 100 to obtain their true cost. This would mean the $2.50 premium on this call option would actually cost you $250 to buy (*$2.50 * 100*).

You decide to buy the option. As the call option buyer, you now have the right to purchase 100 shares of stock XYZ for $50 per share at any time from the moment you buy the option up until the expiration date. If you decide you want the shares *before* the expiration date, you can **exercise** your option. Exercising an option before the expiration date is rare, but still a term you should be aware of. Let's continue with our example.

In one week, on the option expiration date, the market closes and the USP is still above $50; your option has expired *ITM*. When this occurs, the option seller must provide you 100 shares of stock XYZ at $50 a share. Thus, the option has been **assigned** to your account.

If you are the call option buyer and are expecting the option to be assigned, you would need to have enough money in your brokerage account to cover 100 shares of the underlying security at the set strike price. In this example, the strike price was $50, meaning you would need $5,000 in your account to be assigned this option.

In the case where you do not have enough money available, your broker will sell the option automatically briefly before market close on the expiration date. Knowing this, it's important to have the necessary funds in your brokerage account if you are the call option buyer and want to own the stock.

OTM Expiration Example
Stock XYZ is currently trading for $52. An **OTM** call option with a strike price of $54, and an expiration date one week away, trades for $0.30. Buying this option will cost you $30 (*$0.30 * 100*).

When buying an OTM call option, you generally are expecting a large increase in the share price before the expiration date, as the USP must be *higher* than your strike price to make a profit. Technically the USP needs to be higher than the strike price *plus* the premium paid. Take for instance the example we're going over, where the strike price is $54 and the premium paid is $0.30. This would indicate the USP would need to trade for $54.30 on the day of expiration to breakeven on this trade.

Conversely, if upon expiration the USP is *below* $54, this call option expires OTM. This is synonymous with the option expiring "worthless," as nothing else happens at this point. The option seller does not owe you anything, and she keeps the premium you have provided.

As you may be able to gather from this example, selling options can sometimes be a better choice than buying, because when the option expires OTM, the option seller keeps the premium.

What confuses some regarding options is the "100 shares of stock" scenario that goes along with them. New traders may assume you need to have enough in your account to cover the 100 shares at all times. Or they may assume you'll automatically be assigned 100 shares of stock if you buy an option. However, neither of these scenarios need to take place.

Options, like stocks, are *liquid assets* which are tradeable up until expiration. Meaning even if you own an option which is *going* to expire ITM, you can sell it before the expiration date to ensure you are not assigned the option.

This means, as the option buyer, you just need to have enough in your account to cover the price of the option itself, not the full 100 shares of stock. For example, if an option with a strike price of $10 is selling for $0.20, you would only need $20 in your account to buy this option (*$0.20 x 100*).

And so long as you sold the option before it expired, you would never be assigned 100 shares of stock, and thus never need to have $1,000 in your stock account to fund the trade.

Option Expiration Dates

As mentioned previously, there are different types of *expiration dates* tied to options which include the following: weekly options, monthly options, and LEAP options.

Weekly options expire each week, typically on Friday, though some heavily traded ETFs have tri-weekly options which expire on Monday, Wednesday, and Friday.

Monthly options expire on the third Friday of each month. Monthly options tend to have the *most* trading volume associated to them.

LEAP options are a little different; they typically expire on the third Friday of January in the following year, with some stocks and ETFs having even further LEAP options, expiring two or three years into the future.

Option Value

Just a caveat — the information we are about to go over (and have since covered) may seem rather perplexing; this is to be expected when first learning about options. But don't get too bogged down because as you get further in this book and we go over more detailed examples, the information should all come together more fully.

Options are a contract between a buyer and seller which *decay* in value with time. This means each day that goes by, an option is *losing* value. This decay starts to accelerate around 90 days to expiration, with the greatest decay occurring within 30 days to expiration (as shown in the image on the following page).

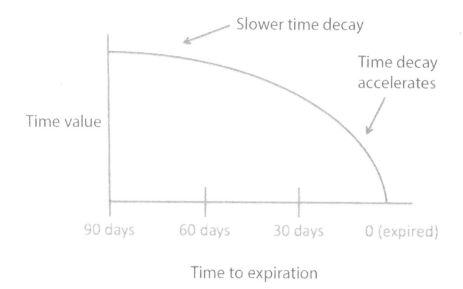

There are two types of values which combine together to determine an option's price (aka premium). These values are called *intrinsic value* and *time value*.

Intrinsic Value + Time Value = Premium

When referencing **call options**, intrinsic value is calculated by subtracting the strike price from the USP. Once you have the intrinsic value calculated, you can now calculate the time value. Time value is calculated by subtracting the intrinsic value from the option premium.

USP - Strike Price = Intrinsic Value
Premium - Intrinsic Value = Time Value

When referencing **put options**, intrinsic value is calculated in reverse, as you subtract the USP by the strike price. Then, like the call option, the intrinsic value subtracted from the full option premium determines the time value.

Strike Price - USP = Intrinsic Value

Premium - Intrinsic Value = Time Value

In either case, neither the intrinsic value nor time value can be negative; they can only go as low as zero. Let's now go over a few examples which will help to better understand this information.

Intrinsic Value Example (ITM)
Stock XYZ is trading for $52 (USP) and you want to buy an ITM *call option* which has a strike price (SP) of $50. In this case, the intrinsic value (IV) would be $2.

$$52 \text{ (USP)} - \$50 \text{ (SP)} = \$2 \text{ (IV)}$$

Intrinsic Value Example (OTM)
Now let's say stock XYZ was again trading for $52, but this time you want to buy an OTM *call option* with a strike price of $54. This call option would have an intrinsic value of $0. While technically it is -$2, intrinsic value cannot be a negative number, as it can only go as low as $0.

$$52 \text{ (USP)} - \$54 \text{ (SP)} = -\$2 = \$0 \text{ (IV)}$$

Time Value Example (ITM)
Let's again look at stock XYZ but, in this instance, also calculate it's *time value* by including the option premium into our example.

As mentioned, stock XYZ is trading for $52. An ITM call option at the $50 strike price, which expires in one week, has a premium of **$2.63**. Using our equation for intrinsic value, we would arrive at the following:

$$52.00 \text{ (USP)} - \$50.00 \text{ (SP)} = \$2.00 \text{ (IV)}$$

The option is currently worth $2.63 though? Where is the extra $0.63 coming from? The answer to this question is the *time value*, considering there is a week left before this option expires.

Each day that goes by, including weekends and holidays, the time value *decreases*. So let's say we came back tomorrow and the USP had stayed exactly the same at $52. Now our option may only be worth $2.53, as its time value has decayed.

Time Value Example (OTM)

Using the same example as above, with stock XYZ trading for $52, let's now go over an OTM call option. Currently, an OTM call option at a strike price of $54 has a premium of **$0.93**. Considering the USP is below the strike price, this call option has no intrinsic value.

$$\$52.00 \text{ (USP)} - \$54.00 \text{ (SP)} = -\$2 = \$0$$

Again, this is because the USP is currently below the $54 strike price, thus making the intrinsic value zero. This means the $0.93 in option premium is strictly comprised of *time value*.

Option Volatility

While intrinsic value and time value are the main aspects of an option's price, volatility can also affect this figure. Volatility would be considered an estimate of where the USP *could* go. Stated differently, the *price range* from now until the option expires.

Many tech stocks and IPOs possess higher volatility than safer stocks such as banks or utility companies. A higher volatility indicates a greater movement in the USP is expected in the future, the direction of which is uncertain.

The two types of option volatility to be aware of are:

1) Historical Volatility (*HV*)
2) Implied Volatility (*IMV*)

Historical volatility is, as the name suggests, the volatility of a particular stock throughout its history.

Implied volatility on the other hand, is an estimate of a stock's volatility at the *present* time and is a more important statistic to reference versus HV.

An example of a stock with a high IMV is Tesla. The price of Tesla is constantly swaying up and down, and there are many short sellers associated with the stock. For these reasons, the future price is rather unpredictable. As such, Tesla options tend to be priced much higher than stocks with the same USP, but which have lower IMV.

This can be more easily depicted in an example where we compare the premium of a Tesla option to that of a company with a similar USP, but a lower IMV.

In the image on the next page, a call option for Tesla (TSLA) is shown on the left, where as a call option for Huntington Ingalls (HII) is shown on the right (HII is a "commercial shipbuilder" whose stock movement tends to be rather minimal).

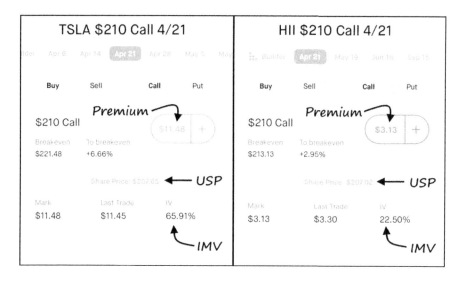

Notice in the image above that both stocks have a similar USP, both call options have the same strike price, and both call options expire on the same date. The only notable difference between these two is their IMV, with Tesla's being much greater. And it is this greater IMV that results in the option premium of Tesla being almost *four times* higher than that of Huntington Ingalls.

While the price action of a stock is one reason for increased IMV, another reason can be an impending company announcement, with the most common example being earnings.

While analysts have estimates, no one knows exactly what financial figures a company will report in any given quarter. Depending on how far off these figures stray from analyst estimates can determine the extent a company's stock price will skyrocket or crash after an earnings report. This uncertainty tends to make options which expire *after* a company's earnings date possess higher IMV, and thus higher premiums, than options which expire *before* the earnings date.

Volume and Open Interest

When you view options in your brokerage account, you will notice two terms which correspond with trader interest in said option:

1) Volume
2) Open Interest

Volume is defined as the number of options contracts which have changed hands on a given day for a specific strike price. For example, let's say an option has an $11 strike price with a premium of $0.35. You put in an order to buy this option for $0.35, which is immediately executed.

Previous to your order, the volume displayed was 705. After your order, the volume displayed is now 706. In other words, 706 options contracts have been exchanged on that day for that strike price.

Open interest is defined as the option orders which are *pending* on that day, for that specific strike price, but which have not yet been exchanged. Let's use the same example as before, with our $11 strike price and $0.35 premium.

The volume currently displayed is 705, while the open interest displayed is 276. You decide you want to buy this option, but for less than the current ask price. You place an order for $0.20, which sits as "pending" with your broker. The volume remains at 705, while the open interest changes from 276 to 277. There are now 277 pending buy and sell orders associated with the strike price of this option.

The greater the open interest and volume of an option, the more liquid it is, and the easier it will be to get in and out of the trade.

Option Greeks

Option Greeks, a concept unique to options, represent statistics related to the option you are trading. Option Greeks tend to be a more advanced field, and you may not even end up using them, but they are still worth understanding.

There are *five* different Greeks, each representing a unique statistic for a given option. A general overview will be provided here, with examples given for each. You will see Greeks touched on throughout the book when we go over option strategies in subsequent chapters.

► **Delta** – represents the change in price of an option premium for every dollar move in the USP. Call option deltas range from 0 to 1, while put option deltas range from -1 to 0.

The closer the delta is to 1 (or -1), the closer the price of the option will move in tandem with the USP. Option deltas became larger the further ITM you move.

▷ *Delta Example: Stock XYZ is currently trading for $20. A call option with a strike price of $17 has a delta of .7105; we'll call this Option A.*

A call option with a strike price of $10 has a delta of .9304; we'll call this Option B.

If stock XYZ increased in price by $1, Option A would increase in price by $0.71, while Option B would increase in price by $0.93.

► **Gamma** - the rate of change of an option's delta based on every dollar movement in the USP. Gamma is commonly known as "the delta of the delta." Gamma tends to be higher ATM, and lessens the deeper ITM or OTM you move.

▷ *Gamma Example: Stock XYZ is currently trading for $20. An ATM call option has a delta of 0.50, and a gamma of 0.10.*

If stock XYZ were to increase in price by $1, the delta would increase to 0.60. If stock XYZ were to decrease in price by $1, the delta would decrease to 0.40.

► **Theta** - the rate of decay in an option's value due to time; also referred to as an option's "time decay" measurement.

▷ *Theta Example: Stock XYZ is currently trading for $20. You buy an ATM call option at a price of $1.50, which has a theta of -0.05. If tomorrow the USP of XYZ remained at $20, the price of the option you* *bought would decrease by $0.05, thus making it now worth $1.45.*

▶ **Vega** - measures the sensitivity of an option to changes in its implied volatility. Specifically, vega measures the increase or decrease in an option premium based on a 1% change in implied volatility. The higher the vega, the more an option price will move when IMV increases or decreases.

▷ *Vega Example: Stock XYZ is currently trading for $20. You buy an ATM call option at a price of $1.50, which has a vega of 0.12 and an IMV of 20%.*

Company XYZ holds a press conference stating big news for their company will be announced the following day. The IMV increases to 22%, a 2% change.

Based on the vega of 0.12, and a 2% change in IMV, the price of the call option would increase $0.24 to $1.74.

▶ **Rho** - measures the expected change in an option price relative to a one-percentage point change in interest rates. In essence, rho tells you the extent an option premium will rise or fall should the "risk-free rate" (Fed-Funds rate) increase or decrease.

Call options are directly correlated to the Fed-Funds rate, while put options are inversely correlated. This means a rise in interest rates would increase a call option premium, while it would decrease a put option premium. This is why calls have positive rho while puts have negative rho.

LEAP options tend to have higher rhos, and are thus more sensitive to interest-rate changes than shorter term options.

▷ *Rho Example: Stock XYZ is currently trading for $20. An ATM call option is priced at $1, and has a rho of 0.25.*

If interest rates rise by 1%, your call option will increase in price to $1.25. If interest rates fall by 1%, your call option will decrease in price to $0.75. These figures would be inversed if you had instead bought a put option.

Free Gift

As a **token of appreciation** to my readers, I am offering my special report titled *Crush the Market* **absolutely free!** In this report, you will learn 18 incredibly beneficial tips that will help you profit in the stock market. Just go to the link below, put in your email address, and the special report will be immediately sent to you!

linkpony.com/crush

Chapter 2
Basic Option Strategies

When you buy a stock, you understand the entity known as the "bid/ask spread." This is the difference between the bid price (*what buyers are offering*) and the ask price (*what sellers are offering*). On most heavily traded stocks, the bid/ask spread is usually just one, maybe two pennies apart... but the option world is much different.

Except for select heavily traded options (*e.g. SPY*), there is usually limited liquidity, and thus larger bid/ask spreads, in the options world. This is especially true the deeper ITM or OTM you move.

The reason for this is because there is much less trading volume with options. Stated another way, you don't have the same amount of buyers and sellers as you do with stocks. This means bid/ask spreads can be 10 cents, 20 cents, 30 cents, or sometimes even more. The price displayed when you look at the option chain is actually the middle of the bid/ask spread.

> *e.g.* *Stock XYZ is currently trading for $50.20. An ATM call option with a strike price of $50, expiring next month, shows a premium of $1.50. When you open the option chain to dig deeper, you find out the bid price is $1.30 and the ask price is $1.70. This means the option currently has a bid/ask spread of 40 cents, and the middle of that spread is $1.50.*

As you may be aware, offering to *buy* this option for $1.70 would allow you to immediately own it. This is because a seller has made an offer in the open market to sell it to you at this price.

The same would be true if you offered to sell this option for $1.30, as a buyer has made an offer in the open market to buy it from you at this price.

However, neither of these trading decisions would typically be appropriate. Instead of matching the bid or ask, you typically want to first try to *split the spread.*

Splitting refers to the act of placing your limit order in the middle of the current bid/ask spread. In our example, this would be an offer of $1.50. When you "split" the spread, two scenarios can occur:

> **Scenario 1:** *Another trader, usually those known as "market makers," will automatically accept the offer you have put forth. And thus, you will now own the option if you bought it (bid), or you will be the option seller if you sold it (ask).*

> **Scenario 2:** *Your offer will sit in limbo. It may take seconds, minutes, or hours to execute. It may never be executed, sitting until the end of the day when it expires. This will all depend on the volume associated with the option and the price action of the USP.*

Let's say a market maker does not automatically accept your trade, but instead scenario two occurs, where your order sits in limbo.

If you chose to **buy** the option, the option price displayed in the open market will change to **$1.60**. This is because *you* are now the highest bidder at $1.50, while the lowest asker is still offering $1.70.

If you chose to **sell** the option, the option price displayed in the open market will change to **$1.40**. This is because *you* are now the lowest asker at \$1.50, while the highest bidder is still offering \$1.30.

The closer to the ask you make your offer as a buyer (*e.g. closer to \$1.70*), or the closer to the bid you make your offer as a seller (*e.g. closer to \$1.30*), the greater the probability your trade will execute.

Pre-Trade Insight

Before establishing any option position, you should first be aware of the following facets of the trade:

- ❖ Max Gain
- ❖ Max Loss
- ❖ Margin Required
- ❖ Breakeven Point

The **max gain** is the most you are able to make on a given option trade. For some trades, such as buying a call outright, the max gain is unlimited. For others, such as a credit-spread, profits become "capped" past a specific USP.

The **max loss** is of course just the opposite of this, being the most you can lose on a given trade. Most trades, especially the more advanced option strategies, have a defined max loss. This makes them somewhat safe as you know you can only lose a specified amount before establishing the trade. A small number of more risky trades, such as selling a naked call, have a theoretical unlimited max loss.

Margin, which we went over in *Chapter 1*, would be additional funds provided to the broker at the onset of the trade. The margin required can differ wildly between trades. Some trades do not have a margin requirement, only encompassing the cost of the option. Others, such as selling a put option, may require the full cost of the strike price (x 100). For example, if you sold a put option with a

$20 strike price, $2000 in margin is required to your broker at the onset of the trade. All or part of this margin is then provided back to you when you close the trade, or if the option expires, a determinate based on the USP.

And lastly, the **breakeven point** is the price the USP must expire in order to not lose any money on a trade. For example, if you were to buy a $20 call option with a $1 premium, the USP would need to expire at $21 to breakeven on this trade (and higher to make a profit). However, this breakeven point only becomes important should your option expire. Many times, traders will close their positions before expiration, in which case the value of the premium and your current profit is the only concern.

Buying an Option

The most basic option strategy would be outright buying a call or put. When you buy an option, the most you can make is infinity, the most you can lose is what you pay for the option, and the breakeven point is the option premium added to the strike price.

If you're going to be outright buying a call or put, you have a few different choices:

1) Weekly Options
2) Monthly Options
3) LEAP Options

The shorter the time period to expiration, the higher the risk. The reason for this is because options decay in value with time, and this is especially true the closer the option moves towards its expiration date.

Conversely, shorter term options offer the highest reward. The closer to expiration, the higher the Gamma and IMV, and the more which can be made in profit should the USP move accordingly.

For example, sometimes after an earnings announcement a stock can jump up in price by say ten percentage points. And with this ten percent increase in the USP, shorter-term call options associated with the stock can go up in value by **hundreds** of percentage points. On the other hand, longer term options (*e.g. LEAPS*) with lower gamma and lower IMV don't move up as dramatically.

That's why weekly and monthly options can be a lucrative gamble, as you can get lucky and make a substantial profit. But that gamble comes with greater risk, because if the USP moves the wrong way, your option expires worthless. Not only that, even if the USP moves in the correct direction, if it does not move *enough* by expiration, you can still end up losing what you paid for the option.

This information infers that if you're going to buy shorter term call or put options, understand that it is akin to gambling. This would mean making small bets, such as if you were going to a casino, is how you should typically position short-term option trades. To rephrase, please do not consider going "YOLO" with your life savings on a short-term options trade (despite what people on Reddit boards may tell you).

If you like a stock for the long-term and are not trying to gamble on earnings, ITM LEAP options tend to be the best option strategy to employ. We will go over this strategy more in *Chapter 5* of this book.

Buying a Call Option

Buying a call option could be compared to buying a stock. What makes it different however is the risk/reward levels, and the fact there's an expiration date associated with your order. Typically people will buy a call option for a two reasons:

1) Gambling on a short-term event (*e.g. earnings*)

2) Investing in a company long term (*e.g. LEAP*)

When buying a weekly or monthly call option, traders hope the stock will rise significantly before expiration. As stated previously, buying a short-term call option *can* pay off, but it's the same way betting on black at the roulette table can pay off. No one knows what price the stock will be an hour from now, let alone a week or a month in the future.

Buying a LEAP call option on the other hand is similar to buying a stock, and thus much safer than a short-term option. With that said, you do not collect a dividend when you own a LEAP, but there are still advantages versus buying a stock outright which can offset this limitation. We'll go over LEAP options more in *Chapter 5*, but for right now let's go over some examples of buying short term call options.

I will be including charts throughout the book, similar to the one below. These charts will help you to visualize trade examples. This first chart is labeled to help connotate what is being displayed.

> ***Note:*** *In the trade examples throughout the book, I will be abbreviating parts of the trade. For example, $20/c represents a $20 strike price using a call option, while $20/p represents a $20 strike price using a put option.*

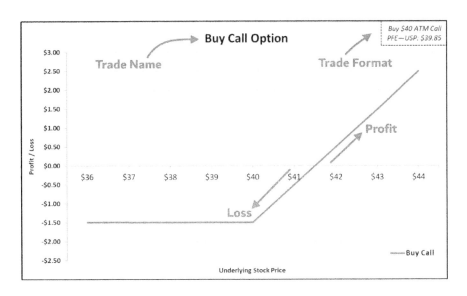

Buying a Call Option: Outline

You arrive in the office on Monday and sneak a look at your phone to check your stock account. You see that Pfizer (PFE) has an underlying stock price (USP) of $39.85 and will be announcing earnings on Thursday afternoon.

When you walk to the break room to get coffee, you overhear a co-worker named Greg who claims to have insider information. He states Pfizer is going to blow analyst estimates out of the water, and he has been accumulating shares.

Based on this information from Greg, you decide to buy an ATM $40/c for **$1.50** which expires on Friday. One hundred and fifty dollars is taken from your cash balance to pay for this option (*$1.50 * 100 = $150*).

The most you can make on this trade is unlimited, while the most you can lose is $150. No margin is held, aside from the cost of the call option. Your breakeven point is $41.50.

▷ Max Gain: Unlimited
▷ Max Loss: -$150

▷ Margin Held: None
▷ Breakeven: $41.50

Scenario #1: Large Gain (Buy $40/c)

After-market hours on Thursday, Pfizer announces higher than expected earnings, greatly beating analyst estimates. By Friday morning, the USP has risen to $48, and your $40/c now trades for **$8.76**. You never intended on owning the stock, but instead just wanted to make a quick buck trading the option.

For this reason, you sell your call option on Friday morning before it expires. You then dance around your house in your underwear and call Greg from the office to tell him he is a stock picking genius.

Your profit is calculated by subtracting the current option premium from your original purchase price.

▷ Result: +$726

Scenario #2: Partial Loss (Buy $40/c)

After-market hours on Thursday, Pfizer announces a normal quarter, matching analyst estimates. On Friday morning, the USP rallies slightly, getting up to $40.07 per share. Most of the IMV dissipates, and your option now trades for just **$0.35**. You decide to sell it before it expires, resulting in a partial loss.

▷ Result: -$115

Scenario #3: Max Loss (Buy $40/c)

After-market hours on Thursday, Pfizer releases terrible earnings and announces they are filing for Chapter 11 bankruptcy. On Friday morning, their stock has tanked to $22.45 per share. Your call option is now trading for just

$0.01. You decide to just let it expire worthless while uttering profanities under your breath about how you could let yourself take stock advice from the bumbling buffoon Greg at the office. You lose the maximum allowable amount on this trade.

▷ Result: -$150

◆ ◆ ◆

There are a few things to grasp from these examples. Buying a short-term call option is cheaper than holding a stock outright, has less risk should the stock tank, and has more reward potential. On the other hand, if the stock stays stagnant until expiration or does not increase enough (as shown in scenarios 2 and 3), you can potentially lose part or all of what you paid for the option.

Buying a Put Option

If you've traded stocks for a bit, you're likely familiar with the concept of "shorting" a stock. This is where you can profit from the decline of a stock by selling the stock before you buy it.

While shorting can be a beneficial way to profit when you think a stock will decline, there are a number of drawbacks you run into such as risk and fees. Put options circumvent many of these disadvantages, while still allowing you to profit when a stock declines in price.

The three advantages of buying a put option versus shorting a stock include:

1) *No shorting fees*
2) *Defined max loss*
3) *Increased profit potential*

When you short a stock, you have to pay fees on said stock for as long as you hold the short. These fees range wildly from 1%-100%+ per year depending on the short demand of said stock. With a put option, while you do have to pay a premium for IMV, there is no "fee" associated with holding it.

Second, you can potentially lose *more* than the amount you originally invest when shorting. For example, if you were to short a $5 stock and it increased to $15, you would now be down 200%. However, a put option can only go as low as $0, meaning you can only lose the amount you originally invest.

And lastly, there is the potential for an increased reward when you buy a put option as opposed to shorting. When you short a stock, the most you can make is your original investment; this is because a stock can only go as low as $0. Conversely, with a put option, you can double or even triple your money if the stock declines enough before the expiration date. This is because the value of the option can increase *greater* than what you bought it for.

Something to note regarding put options is what happens when they expire in-the-money. If you buy a call option and it expires ITM, you are assigned 100 shares of said stock.

However, when you purchase a put option and it expires ITM, you are assigned 100 *short* shares. In other words, you are now shorting 100 shares of stock. Considering this, most traders will simply sell their put option shortly before expiration to avoid assignment.

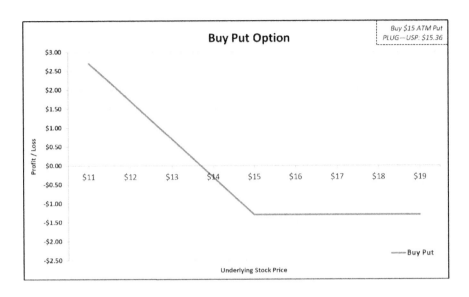

Buy Put Option

Buy $15 ATM Put
PLUG—USP: $15.36

Profit / Loss — Y-axis: $3.00, $2.50, $2.00, $1.50, $1.00, $0.50, $0.00, -$0.50, -$1.00, -$1.50, -$2.00, -$2.50

X-axis: $11, $12, $13, $14, $15, $16, $17, $18, $19

Underlying Stock Price

Buy Put

Buying a Put Option: Outline

Plug Power (PLUG) is currently trading for $15.36. You have a strong feeling this stock has been overbought and thus, is set to decline in the future. You decide to buy an ATM $15/p for **$1.30** which expires in one month.

So far you have $130 invested in this put option. Should PLUG increase in price or stay flat over the next month, the most you can lose is $130. However, your profit limit is essentially uncapped, only limited by the amount PLUG decreases in value by the expiration date.

> ▷ Max Gain: Unlimited
> ▷ Max Loss: -$130
> ▷ Margin Held: None
> ▷ Breakeven: $13.70

Scenario #1: Hefty Gain (Buy $15/p)

Shortly after you buy your put option, a news story is released which alleges insider trading by the CFO of PLUG. This shocking news causes a decrease in the price of the stock.

With 3 days left to expiration, PLUG's USP has declined to $12.20, and your put option premium is now worth **$3.05**. Considering you do not want to short 100 shares of this stock, you decide to sell your put option before expiration.

▷ Result: +$175

Scenario #2: Partial Loss *(Buy $15/p)*
During the month you hold your put option, PLUG stays in a defined range around the $15 mark. On the last day of trading, when your option is set to expire, PLUG is trading for $14.50.

Your put option is currently worth **$0.50**. You sell your option in the open market before the trading day ends, resulting in a partial loss on this trade.

▷ Result: -$80

Scenario #3: Max Loss *(Buy $15/p)*
Two weeks after you buy your put option, the CEO of PLUG announces the company has secured a contract with Chevron to install hydrogen pumps at 1,000 gas stations around the country. The announcement causes the price of PLUG to shoot up past $20 per share.

On the Friday your put option is set to expire, PLUG is trading for $21.20. You decide to let your option expire worthless and lose your initial investment in the option.

▷ Result: -$130

◆ ◆ ◆

With put options, LEAPs are best for stocks you feel will decline long into the future, while shorter term put options are best for gambling on earnings or volatile company announcements.

Selling an Option

Now we get to the other side of the arena: selling options. Every option has a buyer *and* a seller. This means, without owning any part of the stock, you can be an option seller if you choose.

There are three ways most brokers allow you to sell options:

1) *Cash-Secured Puts*
2) *Covered-Calls*
3) *Naked Options*

When you sell a **cash-secured put**, you provide your broker cash up front for the full cost of the put option, which is based on the strike price. Your broker then holds this cash until you close your option position or the option expires. The cash your broker holds is commonly referred to as *margin* or *collateral*.

For example, let's say stock XYZ trades for $43.55. If you sold a $40/p, your broker would set aside a collateral of $4,000 from your cash balance. If you sold two of these options, your broker would set aside $8,000, etc.

This is because the strike price is $40, and you are responsible for purchasing 100 shares of stock, at a price of $40 per share, should your put expire ITM. So the broker is "securing" the funds in the case of assignment. You immediately receive your margin back ($4,000) should you close this position or if the option expires worthless.

A **covered-call** is essentially a cash-secured call, it just goes by a different name. To sell a covered-call, you must first *own* 100 shares of the stock which correlates to the option you are selling. You can then sell a call option on said stock, which is "covered" by every 100 shares you own.

For example, say you buy 100 shares of stock XYZ for $38.50 and then sell a $40/c. You have now sold a *covered-call*, as the call option you sold is "covered" by the stock you own. This way, if the USP should expire above $40 (the strike price of your option), the 100 shares of stock XYZ you own is provided to the option buyer upon assignment.

Naked options, which can refer to both calls and puts, differ in that brokers require much less in initial margin when you initiate the trade. When selling a naked **put** option, 10% of the *strike price* is required as margin. When selling a naked **call** option, 10% of 100 shares of stock, at the *current USP*, is required as margin.

So, as the name suggests, the option is essentially "naked" as only a small portion of money is backing the option in the case it expires ITM.

Let's say stock XYZ is trading for $43.50, and you sell a naked $40/p. Here your broker would only require $400 be set aside while you hold the option (*10% of $4,000 = $400*). This is in sharp contrast to the $4,000 that would be required when selling a cash-secured put.

Let's take the same example, but this time sell a naked *call* option. Here your broker would only require $435 in margin, as XYZ is currently trading for $43.50. And 10% of 100 shares comes out to $435.

As you can tell, there are advantages and disadvantages to both cash-secured and naked options. Not being required to provide so much cash upfront when selling naked options means you can use that cash in other ventures. However, naked options come with the risk of losing money you don't really have, or possibly receiving a "margin-call" from your broker. Contrast this with cash-secured puts and covered-calls, which are considered safer than naked options, but require more cash to initiate.

In either case, after selling an option, there may be times you want to exit your position before the expiration date. Considering you're the option *seller*, to close your position you need to *buy* the option back, also known as "buy to cover" (BTC). If you've ever shorted a stock before, you may be familiar with this term. It essentially means the option is no longer in your portfolio; you are exiting the trade. Since you sold the option first though, you can't "sell" it again, so you BTC to close your position.

Now that we have an overview of option selling, we can go over the specifics of selling calls and puts.

Selling Calls

When you sell a call option, you want the USP to move *down* in value, with the ultimate goal being the stock expiring *below* your strike price. When this occurs, you get to keep the premium provided and the option expires worthless.

In the event a naked call option expires ITM, you are assigned a short stock position of 100 shares, with the average cost being the strike price of the call option. To avoid this scenario, most traders will BTC their call option shortly before expiration if it going to expire ITM.

When researching the max profit/loss potential in regards to selling a call, you'll often see pictures like the one on the next page.

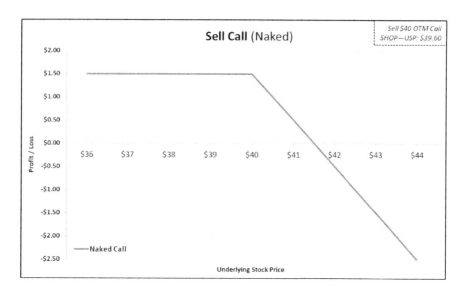

This picture is a visual example of selling a naked call option. As you can gather, there is a limited potential profit with a theoretical unlimited max loss accompanying the trade.

While images like this are helpful for visualization purposes, sometimes these "textbook" images can be deceiving. At first glance, it may seem pointless to partake in a trade with limited profit and unlimited loss potential. However, what textbooks images do not convey is the odds of actually winning or losing on said trade. Or the fact that you can get out of the trade before you lose money. Or that you can trade additional options to mitigate risks.

With all this said, use these images to help you better understand the trade, but don't let the profit or loss potential scare you from actually trying them out. Let's now go over an example of selling a naked call option.

Selling a Naked Call Option: Outline
Shopify (SHOP) is currently trading for **$39.60** and you reckon SHOP will decline in the future. You sell an ATM $40/c, expiring in one month, for $1.50. Considering this is a

naked call option, only 10% of 100 shares (*e.g. $396*) is set aside from your cash balance as margin.

Your max profit is $150, while your max loss is uncapped. The breakeven point on this trade is $41.50. This is due to the premium adding a $1.50 layer of protection above the strike price.

> ▷ Max Gain: $150
> ▷ Max Loss: Unlimited
> ▷ Margin Held: $396
> ▷ Breakeven: $41.50

Scenario #1: Max Gain (Sell $40/c)

In one month, upon expiration, SHOP closes at **$35.42**. Since the USP is *below* the strike price at expiration, the option expires worthless. You receive back your margin ($396), while keeping the option premium, thus making the max profit potential on this trade.

> ▷ Result: +$150

Scenario #2: Partial Gain (Sell $40/c)

In just one week, SHOP has declined to $32. The option premium, which was originally $1.50, now sells for **$0.20**. Considering you are the option *seller*, a decrease in the price of the premium equates to profit in your pocket. You decide to get out of the trade before expiration, meaning you BTC your call option. You receive back your $396 in margin, while making a partial profit on this trade.

> ▷ Result: +$130

Scenario #3: Large Loss *(Sell $40/c)*

In one month, upon expiration, SHOP closes at **$48**. Consider the USP is *above* the strike price at expiration, it has expired ITM.

The cash originally set aside, $396, is not enough to cover what you have lost on this trade; another $254 is needed. Your broker takes these extra funds from your cash balance.

In this scenario, since you are the call seller, on Monday morning you are assigned a short position of 100 shares of stock into your brokerage account at a cost of $40 per share.

While the loss from the strike price ($40) to the USP ($48) is $800, you still get to keep the $150 in premium, which reduces part of this loss.

▷ Result: -$650

As you can ascertain, *Scenario #3* is why selling naked call options can be risky. As the USP moves above your strike price, there is no limit (theoretically) to the amount you can lose. With that said, in the real world stocks don't keep rising forever. Furthermore, you could BTC your option before expiration, thus lessening your losses.

Continuing with selling calls, let's now go over the safer version of this trade: *covered-calls*.

Covered-Calls

Covered-calls are one of the safest options strategies you can implement. The reason why is you can't technically lose money with a covered call (at least not on the option side of the trade), but instead only limit your *potential* profit.

When you sell a call option using a covered-call, you are "covered" from losses by owning said stock in your portfolio. So, if the USP happens to expire above the strike price of the call option you sold, your broker simply sells the stock in your portfolio to cover the trade.

One important factor to be aware of is you must own 100 shares of stock for *each* covered-call option you are able to sell. Let's go over an example selling a naked call option by itself, and then compare it to selling a covered-call.

Say stock XYZ is trading for $60, and you sell an OTM $62/c for $0.50. Upon expiration, every penny above $62.50 ($62 strike + $0.50 premium) is a *dollar* in losses. So if the stock were to expire at $64.00, you would lose $150 on this trade. Conversely, with a covered-call, you would actually make a *profit* in this same scenario.

Here we're going to sell the same $62/c for $0.50 as before, but this time we also *own* 100 shares of stock XYZ. To keep it simple, we will own stock XYZ at an average cost per share of $60 (the current USP).

Upon expiration, the USP is again $64. You've gained $400 from the underlying stock, but have lost $150 from the call option you sold. This equates to a total profit of $250.

Say the stock were to expire at $65. Now you have gained $500 from the underlying stock, but have lost $250 from the call option, again obtaining a profit of $250.

Notice how the stock could expire at $64, or $65, or any other higher number above the strike price, and you would still walk away with the same amount of profit on this trade — $250. All losses associated with the call option are "covered" by the 100 shares of stock you own. You get to keep all profits up to the strike price, *as well as* the premium from the call option you sold. Now let's go over a more detailed example.

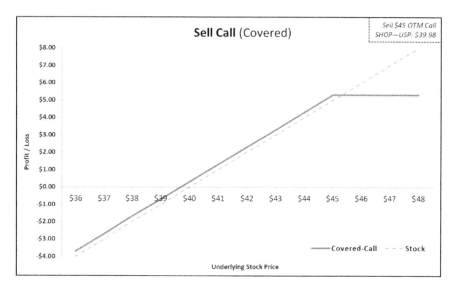

Selling a Covered-Call Option: Outline

You own 100 shares of Shopify (SHOP), which is currently trading for $39.60. For simplicity's sake, your average cost per share is also $39.60.

While you believe SHOP will continue to rise, you do not believe it will get past $45 in one month. You decide to sell an OTM $45/c, expiring in one month, for $0.30. Considering this is a covered-call option, the 100 shares of stock you own acts as the "margin." Also, you can only lose money on the stock you own, not the call option.

> ▷ Max Gain: $570
> ▷ Max Loss: $3,930 *(from the stock)*
> ▷ Margin Held: None
> ▷ Breakeven: $39.30

Scenario #1: Max Gain *($39.60/usp, Sell $45/c)*
In one month, upon expiration, SHOP closes at **$47.11**. Considering the USP is *above* the strike price at expiration, the option has expired ITM and is exercised.

The 100 shares of SHOP you own are provided to the option buyer at $45 per share. You make $540 from an increase in the USP, while also keeping $30 in option premium, thus earning the max potential profit on this trade.

    ▷ Result: +$570

Scenario #2: Partial Gain *($39.60/usp, Sell $45/c)*
In one month, upon expiration, SHOP closes at **$40.42**. You make $82 from the underlying stock price increase of eighty two cents. And since the underlying stock has expired *below* the $45 strike price at expiration, your call option expires worthless, allowing you to keep the $30 in premium.

    ▷ Result: +$112

Scenario #3: Partial Loss *($39.60/usp, Sell $45/c)*
In one month, upon expiration, SHOP has declined to **$39.08**. Since the USP is *below* the strike price at expiration, the option expires worthless. You lose $52 from a decrease in the USP, but keep the $30 in option premium.

    ▷ Result: -$22

As shown in the examples, one drawback of covered-calls is losing out on *potential* profit. Say in one month SHOP closed at $50. Because you sold a call option at a $45 strike price, this is where your profits are capped on the underlying stock. Profits past this number are then covering losses on the call option which you have sold.

However, one benefit of covered-calls is you don't lose as much when the underlying stock price declines, versus strictly holding 100 shares of stock alone. Notice in Scenario #3, even though the stock decreased in value, you didn't lose as much as you *could have* considering you received the premium from the call option you sold.

Covered-calls tend to work best when they are sold one month out and with stocks which you *don't* plan to hold long-term. For example, say you bought stock XYZ at $40, but plan to sell it when it reaches a price of $50. A covered-call will allow you to earn *additional* income each month while the stock is moving towards your target price.

If in one month stock XYZ is still trading below $50, you collect the call premium and can then repeat the process, selling another covered-call one month out. Then when the stock eventually expires above your $50 price target, it is automatically sold for you by your broker.

This equates to taking in "free" money each month, considering you are holding the stock anyway *and* planned to sell it at $50. Such is why many compare selling covered-calls to "renting" out your stock.

With all this said, many people may think, "*Wow, I'll just sell an OTM covered-call on stocks I hold long term and can collect free money on them every month forever!*" And while it sounds good in theory, there is no free money in the stock market.

Nevertheless, there are many books (and charlatans) which capitalize on this myth, proclaiming to traders covered-calls are "free money machines" which can be used on stocks you hold forever. This myth is not true, and is a topic we will discuss further in *Chapter 5*.

In summary, covered-calls can be a good way to make additional money on stocks you already own, but only ones in which you have a target selling price and *don't* plan to hold indefinitely.

One other topic worth mentioning would be the **covered-put**. This is basically the opposite version of a covered-call. Here, you are profiting from stock declines by first *shorting* 100 shares of stock and then selling an OTM *put* option against these shares. While not as commonly used as covered-calls, they are still worth being aware of.

Selling Puts

Selling puts is the same as selling calls, just profiting in the other direction. In other words, you want the USP to *increase* when you sell a put and expire *above* your strike price. Should the USP trade *below* your strike price upon expiration, 100 shares of stock are exercised into your account, with the average cost per share being the strike price.

As mentioned previously, you can choose between implementing a naked-put or a cash-secured put. With both, the amount of money you can lose or gain is the same, with the only difference being how much margin you must provide to your broker when you initiate the trade.

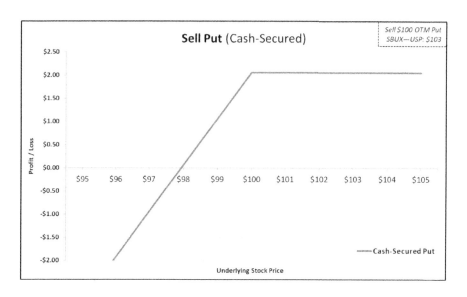

Sell Put (Cash-Secured)

Sell $100 OTM Put
SBUX—USP: $103

Cash-Secured Put

Underlying Stock Price

Selling a Cash-Secured Put Option: Outline

Starbucks (SBUX) is currently trading for **$103**. You can't help but get a venti, mocha Frappuccino with soy milk every morning, and think this stock will rise, or possibly stay flat, over the next month. You decide to sell an OTM $100/p, expiring in one month, for $2.06. Ten-thousand dollars is taken out of your cash balance for margin purposes while you hold this option.

▷ Max Gain: $206
▷ Max Loss: $9,794
▷ Margin Held: $10,000
▷ Breakeven: $97.94

Scenario #1: Max Gain (Sell $100/p)

A month goes by and SBUX closes at **$109.31**, expiring much higher than your $100 strike price. The option has expired worthless. You receive back your margin ($10,000) and earn the maximum profit on this trade. You buy two venti, mocha Frappuccinos the next morning.

▷ Result: +$206

Scenario #2: Partial Gain *(Sell $100/p)*

Two weeks after your initial trade SBUX has climbed to $110 per share. The put option you sold is currently trading for **$0.26**, and you decide to close out your position while you're ahead. You receive back your margin ($10,000) and earn a partial profit on this trade.

▷ Result: +$180

Scenario #3: Partial Loss *(Sell $100/p)*

After one month, upon expiration, SBUX closes at **$95.00**. The stock has expired ITM, as the USP closed *below* your $100 strike price. While there is technically a $500 loss from the USP ($95) to your strike ($100), the premium you initially received helps to recoup part of this loss.

When you open your brokerage account on Monday morning, you are now the proud owner of 100 shares of SBUX at an average cost of $100 per share. You could choose to sell the stock immediately or continue holding your 100 shares until the stock recoups the losses you have incurred. Your Frappuccino spills all over lap as you drive into work.

▷ Result: -$294

As you can tell from scenario #3, when the put option you sell expires ITM, the stock is exercised into *your* account. You then own 100 shares with the average cost being the strike price of your option.

The only difference between a naked put and a cash-secured put is the margin required at the onset of the trade. Had we instead sold a "naked" put in the outline above, only $1,000 would have been held as margin (as opposed to the $10,000). Considering the two are essentially the same trade, it is not necessary for me to go over another detailed example. Just know the two main differences between naked and cash-secured puts:

1) *The amount of cash initially required for margin purposes.*

2) *The fact a margin-call can occur with a naked put should the USP decline significantly upon expiration.*

For these reasons, cash-secured puts are considered safer than naked puts, as the full margin is provided to your broker in the beginning. With that said, naked puts are still fairly safe. The only time they become an issue is when you don't actually have the necessary cash in your account to cover a margin call.

For example, if you were to sell naked puts on a variety of stocks without keeping an adequate cash balance, and then the whole market tanked, you could potentially owe your broker money you don't have. A scenario like this could never occur with cash-secured puts.

Tips on Selling Options
In the past, brokerages used to credit your account as soon as you sold a put or call option. Said differently, if you sold a call option for $0.50, your account would immediately receive the $50 as a credit. In recent times, this immediate credit no longer occurs (as far as I know). Instead, the price of the option rising or falling is reflected in your account balance. Here's an example (margin is not disclosed for simplicity purposes):

e.g. You have $100 in your account and you sell a put option for $0.50 (e.g. $50).

The moment the option is sold, your account balance remains at $100. In one week, the USP has decreased and your put option is now priced at $0.70. If you were to check *your account at this point in time, it would show a balance of $80, as you have lost $20 so far on this trade.*

Another week goes by and the USP has now increased in value, causing the premium on your option to trade for $0.38. If you were to check your account balance at this time, it would read as $112. This is because you are currently up $12 on this trade.

So as long as you hold the option to expiration, you will always end up receiving the full $50 in premium. Depending on where the USP expires however will determine the amount of profit/loss on the trade.

Here's an important fact that differentiates selling puts from selling call options: there *is* a max amount you can lose upon expiration with put options. The price of a stock can only go as low as $0. Meaning if you sell a put option with a $5 strike price and the stock somehow trades at $0 upon expiration (highly unlikely, this is just theoretical), you could lose a max of $500.

Conversely, if we look at selling a naked call option with the same $5 strike price, the stock could theoretically climb to $10, $15, $20, etc. Similar to shorting a stock, you can lose *more* than the amount you initially invest.

All things considered, this hypothetical "unlimited" loss with call options could be alleviated by closing out your option early, selling a covered-call, or using some of the advanced option strategies we will go over in the upcoming chapters.

Rolling Options

Rolling options is a strategy where you believe your trade *will* be profitable, but you need more time for it to pan out. That is to say, your option will soon expire, but you want to remain in the trade by extending the expiration date. There are three ways to roll an option:

• **Rolling Out and Up** - closing your current option position, while simultaneously opening another option position with a later expiration date and a *higher* strike price.

• **Rolling Out and Down** - closing your current option position, while simultaneously opening another option position with a later expiration date and a *lower* strike price.

• **General Rolling** - closing your current option position, while simultaneously opening another option position with a later expiration date and the *same strike price* as your original option.

Which type of "roll" you perform will depend on if you originally sold or bought an option, as well as if you're trading a call or a put.

Rolling an Option You Sold
This trade is typically performed to limit losses when an option is going to expire **ITM**. This can be better understood in an example.

Rolling a Covered-Call: Example
You own 100 shares of stock XYZ, which is trading for $50. You decide to sell a $52 covered-call, expiring in one month, which pays $1.00 in premium.

After one month, on the Friday of expiration, stock XYZ is trading for $55. Your $52 call option now trades for $3.00. Taking into account your initial premium ($100), you are currently down $200 in potential profits on this trade. You have two choices:

A) *Let the Option Expire ITM*
B) *Roll the Option Out and Up*

Choosing *choice A* means the option will expire ITM, which will result in the broker exercising the option and thus taking

100 shares of stock XYZ from your account. You will also lose out on $200 in potential profit.

Choosing *choice B* allows you to potentially regain some of the profit you have forfeited, while also preventing the broker from selling the stock which is covering your call option.

You go with choice B, deciding to roll your option *out and up*. So here you would BTC your current covered-call, while simultaneously selling another covered-call, expiring in one month, at a higher strike price. You choose a $57 strike with a premium of $1.20.

In one month, so long as the USP does not close above $57, you get to continue holding the underlying stock, while also keeping $1.20 in premium. So now, instead of losing out on $200 in missed profits, we have shrunk this figure down to just $80 by rolling our call option out and up.

You would take the same steps had you sold a put option, except you would be rolling your put *out and down*. This is of course because a put option expires ITM when it falls *below* the strike price.

While rolling a short position can be beneficial, there is the risk you can compound your losses even further if the USP continues to move against you. This is particularly true if you are rolling a *naked* call option. With a covered-call, you're not actually losing money, but instead just losing profits you *could* have gained had you only held the stock. Compare this to a naked call, where any movement above the strike price (plus premium) represents a loss in your account balance.

Conversely, rolling a put option (naked or cash-secured), has essentially the same effect should the USP move against you. Both types of put options cause an actual loss to your account balance should they expire below the strike price.

Rolling an Option You Bought

While you can technically roll any option you buy, this process is better reserved for longer term options (*e.g. monthly or LEAPs*), as opposed to shorter term options (*e.g. weekly*). This is because longer term options have more time value associated with them, thus making them cheaper to roll.

Depending on the USP movement prior to the purchase of your option, as well as whether you're trading a put or a call, will determine the type of roll you will perform.

Rolling a Call LEAP: Example

It's a brand new year, and you're a brand new person. You've decided you want to stop losing money in meme stocks and instead will start investing in reputable companies. American Airlines (AAL) is currently trading for $15.82, and you put in an order to buy an ITM LEAP call option with an $8 strike price.

Nine months go by and it is now the middle of October. There is around 90 days left until your option expires, and American Airlines has increased in price over four dollars to $19.98. You would like to continue to hold your LEAP in AAL, but do not want the time value associated with your option to further decay.

You decide to roll your option *out and up*. To do this, you sell your current $8/c (*expiring in 90 days*), while simultaneously buying a $10/c which expires one year later.

You have successfully rolled your call option out and up.

Note: The reason these strike prices were chosen will be elaborated on in Chapter 5.

Rolling a Put LEAP: Example

It is the middle of January and stock CRAP, which recently went through a reverse-split, trades for $50. You remember reading a study called *Long-Run Common Stock Returns following Stock Splits and Reverse Splits*. This study found stocks which undergo reverse splits tend to substantially underperform the market in future years.

Knowing this, you feel stock CRAP will continue to decline into the future. You buy an ATM LEAP put option, expiring in one year, with a $50 strike price.

Some time goes by and, now the middle of October, you have 90 days until your put option expires.

Trading at $50 back in January, CRAP has declined substantially, now trading for just $30. You believe this stock will continue to decline and decide to roll your put option *out and down*. To do this, you sell your current $50/p (*expiring in 90 days*), while simultaneously buying a $30/p which expires in one year.

You have successfully rolled your put option out and down.

How to Beat the Market

A Simple Long-Term Investment Strategy that Beats the S&P 500

Around three decades ago, a little-known study was published that rocked the financial markets. This study proved that you *could* beat the market over the long-term using **one simple strategy**. With data backtested almost 100 years, these findings are hard to ignore. Find out more now at the link below.

linkpony.com/beat

Chapter 3
Advanced Option Strategies

There is a plethora of advanced strategies in the option world. With that said, just because a strategy is more complicated does not mean it is more efficient or that it will result in larger profits.

All advanced strategies involve buying and/or selling multiple options at the same time, and some involve buying/selling as many as 4 options at the same time (*e.g. long call butterfly*). With certain strategies, you're trading all the options on the same expiration date. With others, the expiration date will differ between options. The reason to use each strategy depends on market conditions (*e.g. neutral, bull, bear markets*), USP expectations, and a trader's risk level.

In this chapter and the next, we'll go over a number of advanced options strategies you can use while trading. Then in *Chapter 5*, we'll go over the option strategies that I deem to be the most successful.

Something important to note is when first learning these advanced strategies, it may take some time to fully wrap your head around them. I still have to sometimes stop what I'm doing to fully comprehend how certain strategies work. So don't beat yourself up if you get done with a section and don't fully understand it. I would advise you to learn from this book and then utilize the strategies in a practice account, as seeing them in action will help you to better grasp exactly how they function. The broker Webull offers a free practice options account (linkpony.com/webull).

Credit Spreads

Credit spreads, also called vertical spreads, can be quite a beneficial strategy to employ, especially in accounts with limited funds. A credit spread is essentially a way for you to gain premium from selling an option, while simultaneously buying a lower priced option to limit losses.

There are two different types of credit spreads:

• **Bull-Put Credit Spread** – uses *put* options to create the spread; used when you expect the stock to *increase* in price or remain neutral.

• **Bear-Call Credit Spread** – uses *call* options to create the spread; used when you expect the stock to *decrease* in price or remain neutral.

With a credit spread, as the name implies, you are getting a *credit* when you execute the trade. This is because the option which you are selling has a *larger* premium than the option you are buying. You are no longer selling a "naked" option, as the option you buy actually covers losses should the trade move against you.

The credit spread is considered a directional trade, as you are predicting the USP needs to move in a certain direction before expiration. The highest profit occurs when an ATM strike is sold, while profits diminish the further you move OTM.

The *max profit* potential on a credit spread is the difference between the two option premiums. The *max loss* potential is the difference between the two strike prices, minus the premium received.

The benefits of a credit spread include the following:

1) *Losses are limited*
2) *Minimal capital is needed to implement the trade*
3) *Time is on your side, as you are on the sell side of the trade (e.g. time decay)*

With that said, the disadvantage of a credit spread is your profit is diminished versus selling the call or put by itself. This is because the option you buy when you create the spread cuts into your profit potential.

Let's now go over examples of using both put and call credit spreads.

Bull-Put Credit Spread
Breaking down the title, "bull" signifies you want the USP to increase, while "put" signifies you are using put options to accomplish the trade.

When setting up a bull-put credit spread, you are *selling* an ATM or OTM put option, while *buying* a put option with a lower strike price than the one you sold. For example, say stock XYZ is trading for $20. To set up a bull-put credit spread, you could *sell* a $19/p, while at the same time *buy* an $18/p.

Notice here, the difference between the strike prices is $1, which equates to $100 in the options world. This would mean $100, minus the premium you initially receive, is the most you can lose on this trade. The further you "spread" the strike prices, the greater the risk/reward. For example, if you sold the $19/p while buying the $17/p option, now the most you could lose would be $200 (minus the initial premium). However, a larger payout can now take place as the $17/p is less expensive to buy than the $18/p.

When performing this trade, you are submitting your buy and sell orders simultaneously. With most brokers, this is done by choosing both options before "submitting" the order. Think of it like adding items to your shopping cart before you check out.

Your broker will then show you the bid/ask available on your credit-spread. Here you are setting the limit price and then submitting your order. This process is shown in the image below, in which three items are labeled:

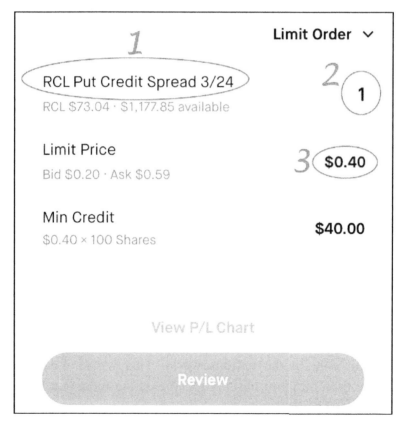

1) Type of Trade
2) Number of Orders

3) The Limit Price

The *type of trade* would be the option trade you are partaking in, which in this case would be a *bull-put credit spread*. Notice too it shows the stock you are trading and the expiration date of the trade.

The *number of orders* is, as the name implies, how many orders you want to initiate. While the image example shows just one, you could of course trade as many credit spreads as you desire, with each additional spread increasing your risk/reward. In this example, one credit spread costs $40, two would cost $80, three would cost $120, etc.

And the *limit price* is what you will be paying for this trade. With a credit spread (and other advanced strategies), the limit price shown is actually a combination of the various options you are trading. But instead of having to buy/sell them individually, the broker combines them into one order, thus executing your entire trade at one time. Notice too in the image that the bid is $0.20 and the ask is $0.59, so the limit price of $0.40 falls right in the middle of these, thus *splitting* the spread.

To maximize your profits with a BPCS, you are aiming for the stock to expire *above* the strike price of the put you sell. Let's go over an example.

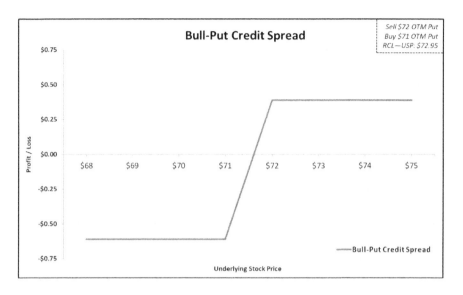

Bull-Put Credit Spread: Outline

Royal Caribbean Group (RCL) is currently trading for **$72.95**. You believe this stock will rise, or possibly stay flat, over the next month. Because you went to Vegas and spent all your savings in the Willy Wonka slot machine, you only have $500 in your stock account. For this reason, you cannot afford to sell a put option outright, as you don't have the necessary funds. However, you *can* perform a credit spread.

You pull up the option chain with your broker, and look for OTM put options which expire in one month. You decide to implement the following:

- Sell **$72/p** for $3.25
- Buy **$71/p** for $2.86

You choose to "split" the bid/ask spread and start the trade with a $39 credit (the difference in premiums). You now have your full bull-put credit spread in place.

A total of $100 is set aside for margin purposes, which corresponds to the difference in the strike prices.

The most you can lose on this trade is $61 (*difference in strikes minus premium received*).

The most you can make on this trade is $39 (*difference in put premiums*).

> ▷ Max Gain: $39
> ▷ Max Loss: -$61
> ▷ Margin Held: $100
> ▷ Breakeven: $71.61

Scenario #1: Max Gain *(Sell $72/p, Buy $71/p)*

Royal Caribbean says they will soon be upgrading their cruise ships with water slides which investors embrace with open arms. RCL increases in price and after one month, it closes at **$74.50**. Both your options have expired worthless, as $74.50 lies *above* the strike price of both put options. You make the maximum allowable profit on this trade.

> ▷ Result: +$39

Scenario #2: Partial Gain *(Sell $72/p, Buy $71/p)*

While you hold your credit-spread, the markets stay flat and no exciting news comes from RCL. After one month, RCL closes at **$71.80**.

Because the stock closed *within* your strikes, but remained *above* your breakeven point, you are able to make a partial profit on this trade.

> ▷ Result: +$19

Scenario #3: Max Loss *(Sell $72/p, Buy $71/p)*

While sailing near Jamaica, a passenger on a Royal Caribbean cruise ship falls overboard and gets eaten by a shark. The news causes RCL stock to go into a tailspin.

A month goes by and RCL closes at **$68.80**. Because the USP closed *below* the strike prices of both of your put options, your full $100 in margin is confiscated by your broker. However, you keep the initial $39 credit you received at the beginning of the trade. You incur the max loss.

▷ Result: -$61

As you may have grasped from this example, much less in margin is required when implementing a credit spread compared to selling a put outright, because the option you are buying *protects* you from losses past its strike price. This means traders with smaller accounts, as well as those more risk adverse, can easily implement credit spreads.

Now let's go over the opposite side of this strategy: a *bear-call credit spread*.

Bear-Call Credit Spread

Again, to break down the title, "bear" signifies you want the USP to decrease, while "call" signifies you are using call options to accomplish the spread.

It is the same as our previous trade, except in reverse. You are *selling* an ATM or OTM **call** option, while *buying* a **call** option with a higher strike price than the one you sold.

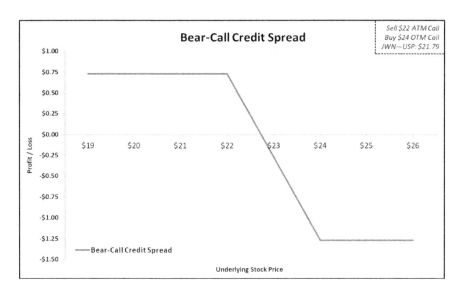

Bear-Call Credit Spread: Outline

The clothing store Nordstrom (JWN) is currently trading for **$21.79**. Over the next month, you believe this stock will stay flat or *decrease* in price. Unfortunately you spent all your money on Amway products which are now sitting in your garage, so you only have $400 in your stock account. For this reason, you decide to open a bear-call credit spread, as it's cheaper than selling a call outright.

You pull up the option chain with your broker and look for call options which expire in one month. You implement the following:

- ► Sell **$22/c** for $1.63
- ► Buy **$24/c** for $0.90

Splitting the bid/ask spread with your limit order, you start the trade with a $73 credit ($1.63-$0.90). Two hundred dollars is taken by your broker as margin to begin this trade ($24-$22).

> ▷ Max Gain: $73

▷ Max Loss: -$127
▷ Margin Held: $200
▷ Breakeven: $22.73

Scenario #1: Max Gain *(Sell $22/c, Buy $24/c)*

The month comes and goes without much press from Nordstrom. The USP ends up declining slightly to **$21.50**, which lies *below* the strike of both of your call options. Your options have expired worthless, the best possible scenario with a credit spread. You receive back your margin ($200) while keeping your initial premium, making the max potential profit on this trade. You use the money to send an email blast to everyone you knew from high school asking them if they want to sign up for Amway.

▷ Result: +$73

Scenario #2: Partial Loss *(Sell $22/c, Buy $24/c)*

A month goes by and the price of JWN rises to **$22.98**. Because the USP closed *within* your strike prices, but ended up *above* your breakeven point of $22.73, you take a partial loss on this trade.

▷ Result: -$25

Scenario #3: Max Loss *(Sell $22/c, Buy $24/c)*

Two weeks after you establish your trade, Macy's announces they will be merging with Nordstrom. The news causes JWN to shoot up in price. On the day of expiration, JWN has risen to **$24.85**.

Because the USP closed *above* the strike of both of your call options, the full $200 in margin is kept by your broker. However, you still retain the initial $73 credit you received. This equates to the max potential loss on this trade. You drink an Amway protein shake as you cry in your garage.

▷ Result: -$127

◆ ◆ ◆

Notice in this example there was a larger difference between the strike prices we bought and sold. Expanding the distance between the strikes increases the amount you can *earn*, while also increasing the amount you can *lose*.

In addition, the further you move OTM with your strike prices, the lower the risk/reward. In other words, you have a better chance of profiting on the trade, but there is less money to be made.

Debit Spreads

Debit spreads are more-or-less the opposite of credit spreads. With a debit spread, you are *buying* the higher priced option, while *selling* the lower priced one. So you start with a debit (*loss*), as opposed to starting with a credit (*gain*).

A debit spread allows you to buy an option, but at a lower cost with the help of the option you are selling. But this lower cost of entry comes with a limited profit potential.

A debit spread is a directional trade, meaning you expect the stock to move higher or lower by expiration. Similar to a credit spread, the highest profit margins occur when you establish an ATM debit spread.

The most you can make on a debit-spread is the difference between the two strike prices minus your initial net debit. The most you can lose on a debit-spread is your initial net debit.

One other point worth mentioning is when **bullish** with debit spreads you're trading *call* options. When **bearish** with debit spreads, you're trading *put* options. This is in direct contrast to the credit spreads we just went over.

Bull-Call Debit Spread

When implementing a bull-call debit spread, you are anticipating the stock will *increase* in value, and ultimately want the stock to expire above the highest strike price in your spread (*the call option you sell*).

For example, let's say stock XYZ is trading for $20. You look at options expiring in one month and buy a call option with a $21 strike price, while selling a call option with a $22 strike price. You have now established your bull-call debit spread.

Considering the option you bought cost more than the option you sold, you are starting this trade with a debit (*net loss*). Should the USP close at or above $22 in one month, you make the maximum allowable profit on this trade. Should the USP close at or below $21 in one month, you lose your initial net debit.

We'll now go over a more detailed example with the stock Alibaba.

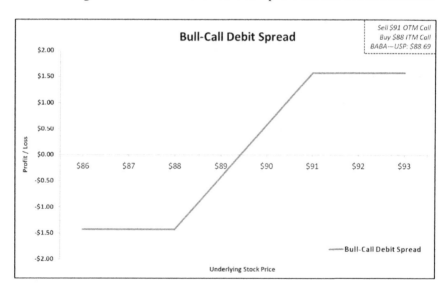

Bull-Call Debit Spread: Outline

Alibaba Group (BABA) is currently trading for **$88.69**. BABA is well down from its highs, and you feel there is a strong case the stock will rebound. With this information known, you decide to open a bull-call debit spread which expires in one month by opening the following positions:

- Buy **$88/c** for $6.68
- Sell **$91/c** for $5.25

You have spent a total of $143 establishing this trade (difference in premiums). The most you can make is $157, while the most you can lose is your net debit of $143.

▷ Max Gain: $157
▷ Max Loss: -$143
▷ Margin Held: None
▷ Breakeven: $89.43

Scenario #1: Max Gain *(Buy $88/c, Sell $91/c)*

Slightly before your option expires, BABA releases earning data which beat analyst estimates. The stock rallies, getting to a price of **$95** by expiration.

Because the USP expired *above* both your call strikes, you earn the max potential profit on this trade. This is calculated by finding the difference in the final intrinsic value of both options ($700-$400), and then subtracting your initial net debit ($143).

▷ Result: +$157

Scenario #2: Partial Gain *(Buy $88/c, Sell $91/c)*

BABA trades mostly sideways throughout the month, rising just slightly to **$90** by expiration. Because the USP expired *within* your strikes, while also remaining *above* the breakeven point of $89.43, you make a partial profit on this trade.

▷ Result: +$57

Scenario #3: Max Loss *(Buy $88/c, Sell $91/c)*

Shortly after establishing your position, rumors swirl throughout the media that Jack Ma, the co-founder of Alibaba, has gone missing. The news causes BABA stock to drop sharply. In one month, upon expiration, BABA closes at **$83**. Because the USP expired *below* both your call strikes, you lose your net debit on this trade.

▷ Result: -$143

Bear-Put Debit Spread

This is simply the opposite of the "bull-call debit spread" we just went over. So instead of using call options, we're now using put options in our debit spread and are betting the stock will *decrease* in value. We'll go over a short example here.

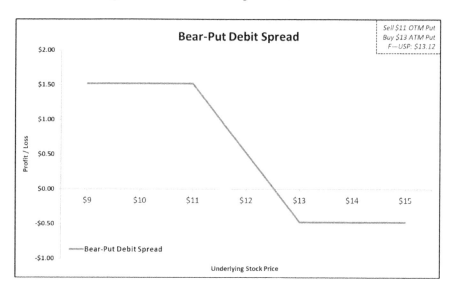

Bear-Put Debit Spread: Outline

Ford Motor Company (F) is trading for **$13.12**. You know Ford stands for "found off-road dead" and believe the stock will decline in the future.

With this foresight, you decide to open a bear-put debit spread on this stock, expiring in one month. You open the following positions:

- ▶ Buy **$13/p** for $0.58
- ▶ Sell **$11/p** for $0.10

You have spent a total of $48 establishing this trade. The most you can make is $152, while the most you can lose is your net debit of $48.

- ▷ Max Gain: $152
- ▷ Max Loss: -$48
- ▷ Margin Held: None
- ▷ Breakeven: $12.52

Scenario #1: Max Gain *(Buy $13/p, Sell $11/p)*

Throughout the month, Ford continues its downward slide and closes at **$10** on the expiration date. Ford has closed *below* the strikes of both your put options, allowing you to collect the max profit on this trade.

This is calculated by finding the difference in the final intrinsic value of both options ($300-$100), and then subtracting your initial net debit ($48).

- ▷ Result: +$152

Scenario #2: Partial Gain *(Buy $13/p, Sell $11/p)*

Over the next month, Ford's stock stays range bound, declining slightly to **$12** by the expiration date. Because the USP expired within your strike prices, while staying *below* your breakeven point, you make a partial profit on this trade.

- ▷ Result: +$52

Scenario #3: Max Loss *(Buy $13/p, Sell $11/p)*

Three weeks after you open your position, surprise sales figures come out showing Ford has the best-selling truck in America. The news pushes up Ford's stock, closing at **$14** by expiration. The USP has expired *above* both your put option strikes, meaning you lose your total net debit on this trade.

▷ Result: -$48

As you may have noticed, credit and debit spreads are quite similar. Here is best analogy I can offer for when to use a debit spread versus a credit spread:

- If you think the USP *will* move past a certain price, use a debit spread.
- If you think the USP *won't* move past a certain price, use a credit spread.

Scourer the internet and you'll find there really isn't a direct science in terms of whether to use a credit or debit spread, but rather it comes down to personal preference of the trader. Knowing this, try out both in a practice account to help you determine which you favor more. The only other information I'll note is time decay works *in your favor* with a credit spread, while it does not with a debit spread.

Long Straddle

A long straddle is considered a "directional" option trade, in that you are betting the stock will undergo significant movement by expiration. However, unlike other strategies, you *do not* need to predict which way it will move, as either direction results in a profit.

This strategy involves buying a call and put option at the same time, both with the same ATM strike price and expiration date. A straddle tends to be used just prior to a big company announcement, with earnings being the most common example.

The theory is the announcement will cause a large rise or decline in the stock price. And regardless of which way the stock moves, so long as it moves enough, you will make money using a long straddle.

The most you can make with a long straddle is infinity, and the most you can lose is the initial cost of your put and call options.

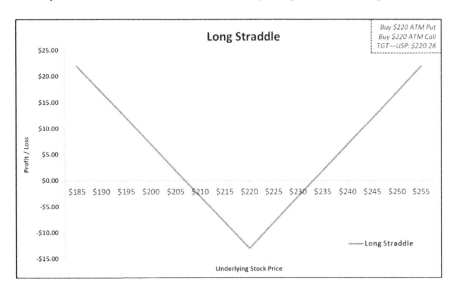

Long Straddle: Outline

It is Tuesday and Target Corporation (TGT) is trading for **$220.28**. The economy has been volatile recently, and Target is posed to announce earnings tomorrow morning, though no one is sure how well (or poorly) they have done this quarter.

With this information known, you decide to open a long straddle which expires at the end of the week (Friday).

- ▸ Buy $220 **call** for $5.35
- ▸ Buy $220 **put** for $7.70

You have spent a total **$1,305** establishing this trade, which is also the most you can lose. On the other hand, there is no cap on the profit potential. The breakeven points are the total cost of both your options ($13.05) above and below $220.

- ▷ Max Gain: Unlimited
- ▷ Max Loss: -$1,305
- ▷ Margin Held: None
- ▷ Breakeven: $206.95 / $233.05

Scenario #1: Large Gain *(Buy $220 C+P)*

Premarket on Wednesday, TGT announces they had a blowout quarter and beat analyst earnings estimates many times over. When the market opens at 9:30am, TGT is trading for **$235.22**.

Your call option is valued at $22.35 while your put option is worth $0.00; you decide to immediately close both positions. You make $1,700 on your call option, while losing the full cost of your put option, $770.

- ▷ Result: +$930

Scenario #2: Partial Loss *(Buy $220 C+P)*

Not much information comes from TGT's earnings call, being mostly eventless. When the market opens at 9:30am, TGT has declined slightly to **$218.25**. Your put option is trading for $5.85 while your call option is worth just $1.05. You decide to immediately close both positions, taking a partial loss on the trade.

- ▷ Result: -$615

Scenario #3: Large Gain *(Buy $220 C+P)*

On the premarket earnings call, Target's CEO begins to cry when he announces dismal quarterly earnings. When the market opens at 9:30am, TGT has crashed down to $163.07. You decide to wait to see how the day will progress before closing out your trade. By day's end, TGT has continued its decline, now trading at just **$161.61**.

By this time, your call option is worth $0.00, while your put option has climbed to a whopping $53.50. You decide to close both your positions minutes before the closing bell.

▷ Result: +$4,045

With this strategy, you want to buy options which are going to expire *after* the company announcement, but which are as close to this date as possible. For example, if earnings are announced on a Tuesday, you would want to buy options expiring that Friday. The closer to expiration, the cheaper the options, and the less it will cost you to implement this trade. Longer term options just end up costing more and don't really add any value in terms of profits.

Furthermore, you want to sell both options as soon as possible after said company's announcement. There are two reasons for this:

1) *Stocks tend to revert to their mean the longer you wait after a volatile announcement.*

2) *Time decay will weigh on the price of your options the longer you hold them.*

A *long straddle* tends to be best used with highly volatile stocks where earnings or other announcements can cause major swings in the stock price. And while IMV causes both the put and call premiums to rise *prior* to the earnings announcement, a profit can still be made with enough movement in the USP (as shown in scenarios 1 and 3).

However, as revealed in scenario #2, you can end up losing a large part of your initial investment should there be little movement in the USP following earnings. This is because IMV greatly decreases after earnings are announced, especially if the earnings are lackluster in nature.

You may have noticed this strategy is called a long straddle. There is another version of this trade called a *short straddle* where you **sell** an ATM call and put option. With a short straddle, you are anticipating little movement in the USP, as the closer it stays to your strike prices, the better.

But due to the unlimited risk potential, the short straddle is a particularly dangerous trade to partake in. Granted, this risk can be alleviated when made into a "butterfly," a trade which will be further touched on in *Chapter 4*.

Long Strangle

A *long strangle* is very similar to the long straddle, with the difference being the placement of your strike prices. With this trade, you are moving your call/put options from "at-the-money" to "out of the money." In other words, you are widening the strikes.

Moving the option strikes further away from the USP decreases the cost of entry, but in turn requires a *more* dramatic move after earnings for a profit to be obtained.

The most you can make on a long strangle is unlimited, and the most you can lose is the initial cost of your put and call options.

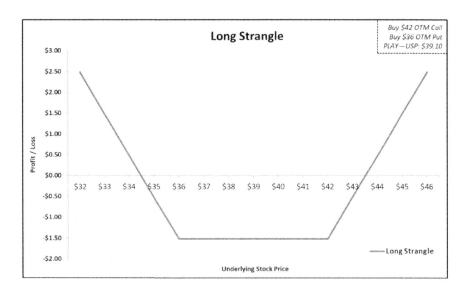

Long Strangle: Outline

It is Monday and Dave & Buster's (PLAY) is currently trading for **$39.10**; they will be announcing earnings tomorrow morning. You love going to Dave & Buster's to get drunk and whoop on 8 year olds at Mario Kart. You've heard great news and expect them to crush their earnings this quarter. Considering this, you decide to implement a *long strangle*.

With $39 being ATM, you pull up the options chain to view strike prices which are $3 away and expire on Friday. You decide to buy the following:

- ► Buy $42 **call** for $0.76
- ► Buy $36 **put** for $0.76

You now have a full strangle in place and are ready for the earnings report tomorrow morning. Your profits are uncapped while your max loss is the cost of the options, $152. Your breakeven points are $1.52 below your put and above your call.

▷ Max Gain: Unlimited
▷ Max Loss: -$152
▷ Margin Held: None
▷ Breakeven: $34.48 / $43.52

Scenario #1: Small Gain *(Buy $42/c, $36/p)*

On the earnings call Tuesday morning PLAY announces they have beat analyst estimates in all categories and their stock shoots up in value.

Near the closing bell on Tuesday, PLAY is trading for **$45.25**. Your $42/c is valued at $3.65, while your $36/p is worth $0.01. You close out your call option while letting your put expire worthless.

▷ Result: +$213

Scenario #2: Partial Loss *(Buy $42/c, $36/p)*

On Tuesday morning, PLAY beats earnings estimates but the stock doesn't seem to move much, rising to just **$40.25** by the end of day. Your $42/c is valued at $0.33, while your $36/p has declined to $0.10. You close out both of these positions shortly after the opening bell, taking a partial loss on this trade.

▷ Result: -$109

Scenario #3: Large Gain *(Buy $42c, $36/p)*

Premarket Tuesday morning, the CEO of Dave & Buster's announces that he has secretly been rigging the financial statements and D&B's is actually in massive financial debt. Flabbergasted by the news, traders sell PLAY stock in droves.

By end of day Tuesday, the USP is trading for **$29.45**. Your $36/p is valued at $11.20, while your $42/c is worth $0.00.

You close out your put while letting your call expire worthless.

▷ Result: +$968

Notice in these scenarios, where earnings are announced pre-market, you are closing both your positions on that same day (or at least closing one to let the other expire worthless).

In a scenario where earnings are announced in the afternoon (after market close), you would sell the next day. The reason why is, after a big move, there is still some time value left in your option that you can capitalize on by selling.

Also, these huge moves after earnings announcements are sometimes short lived, meaning the stock price could revert back to its mean after a few days. In most circumstances, it is better to get rid of both options as soon as the earnings are over, as opposed to waiting until the option expires.

Notice the title of this trade is a long strangle. There is another version of this trade known as a *short strangle*, where you are **selling** a call and put option with wide strike prices. A short strangle is used when you expect a neutral outlook on said stock. Put another way, you expect little movement in the stock price after an earnings announcement.

With a *short strangle*, so long as the USP doesn't expire above or below your strike prices, you keep the premium from both options you sold. However, your short positions are not covered, making the short strangle a rather risky trade. A less-risky version of the short strangle is known as an *Iron Condor*, which we will cover later in the book.

Poor Man's Covered Call (PMCC)

Maybe you want to trade a covered-call option, but lost all your money investing in Dogecoin? Have no fear, you can always entertain a poor man's covered call.

As the name suggests, this is technically a covered-call, but you don't actually own the underlying stock. Instead, you are buying an ITM call option, while also selling an OTM call option. This allows you to enter a "covered-call," but at a discounted price versus buying 100 shares of the stock outright.

While you can find a variety of suggestions online of how to accomplish this trade, the strategy recommended below is the most common.

Rule #1: *ITM Call ≥ 120 Days Expiration*

You want the call option you buy to have a far expiration date to help prevent time decay. As stated earlier in this book, time decay tends to accelerate < 90 days until expiration. So the further in time to expiration, the better. Also, if you bought a *short-term* call option that were to expire ITM (a likely scenario), you would now need the cash to purchase 100 shares of stock, the very affair you were trying to avoid with a PMCC.

Rule #2: *ITM Call Delta > 0.80*

A delta greater than 0.80 provides a better dollar for dollar match when the trade moves in your favor. Meaning you won't just make money from the call option you sold, but also the ITM call option you are buying.

Rule #3: *OTM Call Expires in One Month*

You want the call option you sell to be near-term, with one month being the most commonly chosen expiration. This length of time provides the best value, while also experiencing rather rapid time decay, a benefit when you are the option seller.

Notice rule number two requires a delta greater than 0.80. Delta is directly correlated with how "deep" ITM you purchase the call. In other words, the further ITM you go, the higher the delta on the option. And while an ITM call will be more expensive than an ATM call, it still is a substantial discount versus buying 100 shares of stock outright.

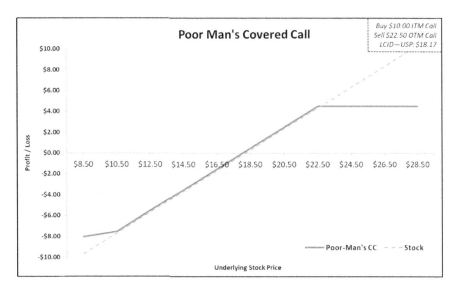

Poor Man's Covered Call: Outline

Lucid Motors (LCID) is presently trading for **$18.17**. You believe that LCID will move higher, but stay below $22.50 over the next month. You decide to open a poor man's covered call by implementing the following:

▶ **Buy** ITM $10 call for $8.50 which has a delta of 0.9371 and expires in seven months

▶ **Sell** OTM $22.50 call for $0.48 which expires in one month

You now have a full PMCC implemented at a cost of $802 (*implementing a real covered-call would have cost you $1,769*). The most you can make ($450) includes stock appreciation to the $22.50 strike, as well as your $48 premium. The most you can lose is $802 (this is just on paper though; the stock would need to become $0).

  ▷ Max Gain: $450
  ▷ Max Loss: -$802
  ▷ Margin Held: None
  ▷ Breakeven: $17.69

Scenario #1: Max Gain *(Buy $10/c, Sell $22.50/c)*

One month goes by and on Friday, 30 minutes before the closing bell, LCID is trading for **$23.00**. The $22.50/c you sold is trading for $0.50, while the $10/c you bought is worth $13.02.

Because your $22.50/c is ITM and you want to avoid assignment, you BTC this option before the market closes.

You are now left with your $10/c and can repeat this process over the next month if you choose. You make the max allowable profit on this trade.

  ▷ Result: +$450

Scenario #2: Partial Gain *(Buy $10/c, Sell $22.50/c)*

After one month LCID closes at **$22.00**. The OTM $22.50/c you sold has expired worthless and the $48 in premium is kept.

You also make $358 from the appreciation of your ITM call option. This is calculated by multiplying the delta of 0.9371 by the actual increase in the USP ($383). You make a partial gain on this trade.

  ▷ Result: +$408

Scenario #3: Partial Loss *(Buy $10/c, Sell $22.50/c)*
One month comes and goes and LCID has decreased in value to **$17.00**. Your $22.50/c has expired worthless, allowing you to keep the $48 in premium.

However, your ITM call option has lost $108 in value. This is calculated by multiplying the delta of 0.9371 by the actual loss of the USP ($117). You take a partial loss on this trade.

▷ Result: -$60

Just like a covered-call, so long as the stock stays flat or rises in value, you make money on this trade. Despite this, there are three small drawbacks using a PMCC versus a regular covered-call:

1) *Time decays the value of your ITM call option.*

2) *You're not making a true dollar for dollar match when the stock price rises.*

3) *Getting out of your ITM call option may be difficult if it has a large bid/ask spread.*

With this said, you essentially get the same risk/reward versus a regular covered-call, while only having to shell out about half of the money you normally would. Also, the deeper you go with your ITM call option, the higher the delta, and the closer you get to the same reward as a normal covered-call.

ReInvent the Wheel

A Low-Risk Options Strategy that Generates Income Three Ways Every Month

The wheel was originally developed in 4000 BC in ancient Mesopotamia... it's time to reinvent it! In *Reinvent the Wheel*, Tim Morris shows you how to combine stocks and options to generate income **three different ways** each & every month. Find out more now at the link below!

linkpony.com/wheel

Chapter 4
More Advanced Option Strategies

We are now getting into the more advanced option strategies. These are the trades that may require different strike prices, different expiration dates, and/or greater than two options to implement. Something to note is just because these are "more advanced" strategies does *not* mean they are superior or will make you more money than the ones we have previously gone over. Much of option trading comes down to personal preference and how well a trader does with any given strategy.

Like the strategies in the last chapter, you implement these trades by submitting all your orders simultaneously. You do this by choosing each option you want to trade and then submitting one limit order price which establishes the entire trade.

Iron Condor

An iron condor is a neutral, non-directional option strategy where you are betting the USP will remain in a pre-determined range until expiration. Thus, you are gaining a profit from the *time decay* of the options you sell.

An iron condor involves implementing four option orders, all of which expire on the same date (generally one month out).

Remember our credit spreads from *Chapter 3*? The Iron Condor is just two credit spreads at the same time:

- ▶ One OTM *bull-put* credit spread
- ▶ One OTM *bear-call* credit spread

Then, should the USP expire in-between these two spreads upon expiration, you receive **two** net credits as a profit on this trade.

The most you can make on this trade is your two net credits. The most you can lose is one strike spread minus your two net credits (this loss tends to be rather limited though, even more so than a regular credit spread due to the fact you get a second net credit and only one spread can lose value upon expiration).

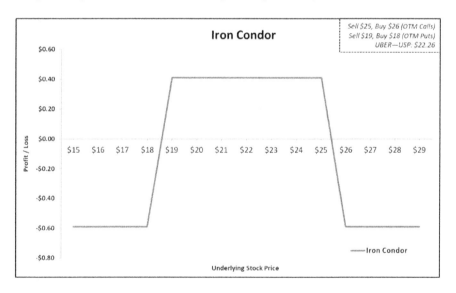

Iron Condor: Outline

You open your brokerage account to find Uber Technologies (UBER) trading for **$22.26**. You believe UBER will stay in a

$6 price range over the next month and thus decide to open an iron condor.

To start, you would implement an OTM *call spread* by:

- Selling an OTM $25/c for $0.65
- Buying an OTM $26/c for $0.44

Here you earn a net credit of $21 and have the first leg of your iron condor. Next, you implement the OTM *put spread* by:

- Selling an OTM $19/p for $0.67
- Buying an OTM $18/p for $0.47

Here you earn a net credit of $20 and the second leg of the condor complete. You now have your **full** iron condor in place which expires in one month.

▷ Max Gain: $41
▷ Max Loss: -$59
▷ Margin Held: $100
▷ Breakeven: $18.59 / $25.41

Scenario #1: Max Gain ($18/$19p, $25/$26c)
Over the next month, the market remains uneventful, trading mostly sideways. UBER ends up closing at **$21.83**. This final price is between your $18/$19 and $25/$26 spreads. Thus, all your options have expired worthless, and you make the maximum profit on this trade.

▷ Result: +$41

Scenario #2: Max Loss ($18/$19p, $25/$26c)
Two weeks go by and UBER announces they will be releasing self-driving taxis in major cities across the United States. This announcement causes a rally in the stock price.

By the time your options expire, UBER is trading for **$27.02**. While your put options expired worthless, your call options did not. Taking into account the $100 you lost from your call option spread, and factoring in your initial $41 net credit, you incur the max loss on this trade.

▷ Result: -$59

While the trade example we went over would be a common method to implement an iron condor, there are a variety of ways you could modify your set-up. You could place one of your spreads closer to the USP if you want to make this more of a "directional" trade. You could widen the strikes. You could extend the expiration dates. Etc.

The iron condor tends to have a high win rate, especially the further you move OTM with your call/put option spreads. The only issue you face with this trade is big market swings, in which case you incur the max loss. Nevertheless, due to its defined risk/reward factors, the iron condor is a rather safe trade to implement when trading options.

Long-Call Butterfly
While there are a variety of butterfly trades which can be performed, we will just be going over a *long-call butterfly* in this section. Other butterflies, such as the short put butterfly, reverse iron butterfly, etc., are just a variation of the long call butterfly trade.

The long-call butterfly involves a total of 4 options, all of which are **call** options:

- ► Buy 1 OTM Call
- ► Sell 2 ATM Call

► Buy 1 ITM Call

A butterfly is a neutral, non-directional trade which realizes its profits from *time decay*. The max potential profit occurs at one specific price point (ATM), becoming less the further the USP moves away from this point. This makes the butterfly a more difficult trade to accomplish, but one which has a high reward and low risk potential should it be implemented effectively.

Another advantage to this trade is how little in collateral is held upfront, with just the initial "net debit" taken by your broker to implement the trade. And in the example we will go over below, this equates to a net debit of just $9, with a potential profit of $91. This low risk, high reward scenario is common with the butterfly trade.

The most you can make on a butterfly is the distance from your ATM leg to your OTM leg, minus your initial net debit. The most you can lose on a butterfly is your initial net debit.

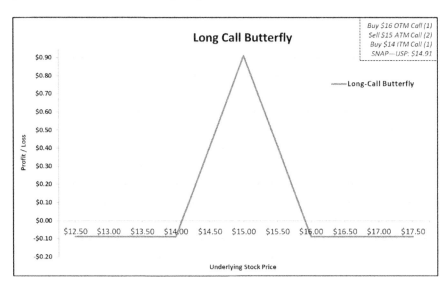

Long-Call Butterfly: Outline

Snapchat (SNAP) is currently trading for **$14.91**. You really like making trendy dance videos on TikTok that get 10 views and think Snapchat is old news. You believe that SNAP will stay close to $15 over the next month and decide to open a long-call butterfly spread.

You add the following options into your trade, all of which are calls, and have the same Friday expiration date one month away:

- ▶ Buy **one** OTM $16/c for $1.47
- ▶ Sell **two** ATM $15/c for $1.90
- ▶ Buy **one** ITM $14/c for $2.42

You click submit and now have your full long-call butterfly in place, starting with a net debit (loss) of $-0.09. This is calculated by adding the two options you bought, while subtracting the two options you sold. This $9 is also *all* that is required to implement this trade *and* the most you can lose.

- ▷ Max Gain: $91
- ▷ Max Loss: -$9
- ▷ Margin Held: None
- ▷ Breakeven: $14.09 / $15.91

Scenario #1: Max Gain *(Sell two $15/c, Buy $14/c + $16/c)*

Over the next month, SNAP trades mostly sideways, expiring at exactly **$15.00**. Your OTM $16/c expires worthless, while your ITM $14/c expires $1 ITM. You also keep the premiums from the two $15/c's you sold.

While you lost $2.89 from the two options you bought, you gained $3.80 from the two options you sold. However, just notating the big picture that the USP expired exactly on the

ATM strike price of $15, you would know you made the max potential profit on this trade.

▷ Result: +$91

Scenario #2: Partial Gain *(Sell two $15/c, Buy $14/c + $16/c)*
After a month, SNAP has moved slightly higher, expiring at **$15.50**. Without doing any math, you know that so long as the USP expires within 91 cents on either side of $15 (ATM), you make a profit on the trade. And since it expired fifty cents above the ATM strike, just subtract $50 from $91 (max-profit), and you get your winnings on this trade.

▷ Result: +$41

Scenario #3: Max Loss *(Sell two $15/c, Buy $14/c + $16/c)*
A short time after you implement your trade, the CEO of SNAP announces on an earnings call that they are losing substantial userbase to TikTok dance videos. The stock freefalls to $11, before bouncing slightly to close at **$13.55**. The USP expired outside of your strike price range, resulting in the maximum loss on this trade — your initial net debit.

▷ Result: -$9

As you can see from these examples, the long call butterfly can be a low risk, high profit trade. The main issue we run into however is we're trying to predict, with almost certainty, the exact price the stock will be at some point in the future — a highly uncertain forecast. For this reason, implementing this trade perfectly can be rather difficult. Nevertheless, you could have performed our trade example 10 times, and if just one expired ATM, you would still be in the green.

While the example we went over is a typical butterfly, you could move your OTM and ITM strikes further away from your ATM shorts. This movement increases your profit potential, increases the likelihood the trade will expire within the strike prices, but also increases your initial net debit.

Long-Call Calendar Spread

Similar to the butterfly, a calendar spread realizes its profits from *time decay*. With a calendar spread, you are again trying to predict the price a stock will expire at a *future* date, with the profit potential decreasing the further the USP moves from this price. Here we will just be going over a *long-call calendar spread*, however there are other versions of this trade which include a long-put calendar spread and a short-put calendar spread.

To start, you choose a price you think the stock will trade at some point in the future (*e.g. one month out*). This price could potentially be the same (*e.g. ATM*) or higher than the current USP. You then use this price as the target for the call option you are *selling*, which is called the "front-month" option. The front-month option is typically one month away from the current date.

After this, you are going to buy a call option with the *same* strike price, but a *further* expiration date, typically two months out. This is known as the "back-month" option. Your calendar spread trade should look something like this:

- ▶ **Sell** 1 ATM Call, one month out (*front-month*)
- ▶ **Buy** 1 ATM Call, two months out (*back-month*)

The goal of this trade is for your front-month option to expire worthless, at which point you close out your back-month position. In other words, you are holding this trade until the nearest call option expires and then closing your 2nd position.

With a calendar spread, you start with a net debit (loss), which ends up being the most you can lose on the trade. The most you can make on the trade is the premium from the front-month option, plus the remaining value of the back-month option when you close out your position.

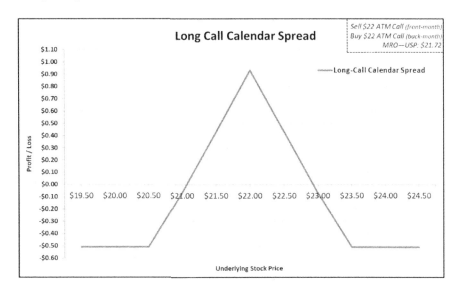

Long-Call Calendar Spread: Outline

Marathon Oil (MRO) is currently trading for $21.72 and you believe it will stay close to $22 over the next month; you decide to open a calendar spread.

To implement this trade you:

- ► **Sell** one ATM $22/c for $1.44 (*front-month*)
- ► **Buy** one ATM $22/c for $1.95 (*back-month*)

You now have a full calendar spread in place, starting with a net debit of -$0.51. The most you can lose on this trade is your net debit. The most you can make will be around $93. This is calculated by taking the premium you will receive from the front-month option ($1.44) and then estimating the remaining worth of the back month option upon expiration.

▷ Max Gain: $93
▷ Max Loss: -$51
▷ Margin Held: None
▷ Breakeven: N/A

Note: The max loss stated is only applicable if you sell the back month option after the front month option has expired. If you choose to keep holding the back month option, your max loss can be greater.

Scenario #1: Max Gain *(Sell $22/c-front, Buy $22/c-back)*

In one month, MRO closes exactly at **$22.00**. Your front-month call option has expired ATM, synonymous with worthless, allowing you to keep $1.44 in premium. Your back month call option is trading for $1.43, which you immediately close. Due to the fact the USP expired ATM, you make the max allowable profit on this trade.

▷ Result: +$92

Scenario #2: Partial Gain *(Sell $22/c-front, Buy $22/c-back)*

MRO rises slightly over the next month, expiring at a price of **$23.00**. Your $22 front month call option (*short*) has lost $1.00 of value. Your back month call option (*long*) currently trades for $1.98. You close out both your positions shortly before the trading day ends, resulting in a partial profit on this trade.

▷ Result: +$47

Scenario #3: Max Loss *(Sell $22/c-front, Buy $22/c-back)*

News breaks that Saudi Arabia has broken ground on a new oil reserve, containing as much as 100 billion barrels of oil. This news causes the price of oil to plunge, and by the time your option expires, MRO is trading at $14.02.

Your front month option expires worthless, while your back month option is now trading for just $0.01. You decide to just let both options expire worthless, losing your net debit on this trade.

> ▷ Result: -$51

◆ ◆ ◆

Calendar spreads have a pretty wide range in which you can make a profit, even if you're wrong on the exact price the front month option will expire.

Advanced Strategies - Additional Insights

As mentioned at the beginning of this book, there is typically *less* trading volume in the options world. With this known, the issue with some of these "advanced" strategies is the large bid/ask spreads — an issue which textbooks don't take into account.

For example, let's say you want to *buy* a call option that sells for $1.15, but has a $0.30 bid/ask spread. And then let's say you weren't able to split the spread, thus forced to buy at the ask price of $1.30... as soon as you enter the trade, you're already down $0.15. This may be okay with one option, because if your strategy works out, you'll make the money back.

On the other hand, if your initial trade involves entering four option contracts, and you have trouble splitting the bid/ask spread with each one, this presents big issues monetarily. You are now down $0.60 at the onset of the trade.

For this reason, you want to make sure you're trading options with high liquidity and low bid/ask spreads if you plan to use any of these advanced strategies.

Customer Reviews

⭐⭐⭐⭐⭐ 38

4.8 out of 5 stars ▾

5 star		87%
4 star		10%
3 star		3%
2 star		0%
1 star		0%

See all 38 customer reviews ›

Share your thoughts with other customers

Write a customer review

If you are enjoying this book, could you please leave a review on Amazon? It would be greatly appreciated and allow me to come out with more informative books in the future. A shortened link to the review page is below:

linkpony.com/options

Bonus Chapter
Favorite Option Strategies

The sad fact is most option traders (and stock traders for that matter) lose money. We sometimes see stories on the internet of a trader using options to make thousands of dollars in a matter of days, or even hours, and then decide we want to get in on the action.

What we may fail to realize however is the many *more* traders who have lost thousands (millions?) trading options. These are the people who take out home equity loans, max out their credit card advances, or use the broker allowed margins to try and get rich quick, almost always resulting in the opposite outcome.

For this reason, I tend to shy away from options strategies which are pure gambles (*e.g. weekly calls*), or where you are not only trying to predict a future price, but *also* trying to predict the exact date it will occur (*e.g. calendar spreads*). Moreover, some of the advanced option strategies require multiple orders, up to 4 in some cases, which can be quite hard to implement (and be successful) when there is limited liquidity and you can't split the spread.

While I still sometimes use these strategies, I trade them using limited funds, knowing full and well I am simply gambling. In other words, I only use money I can *afford* to lose and which will not keep me up at night.

The option trades I prefer more, and which I use more often, are lower risk strategies. Ones which do not require you to be a psychic and know the exact price the stock market will trade on a future date. Strategies which require just one, at most two orders to implement. With this in mind, here are my favorite option strategies.

Selling Puts

What is so worthwhile about selling puts is the many different scenarios the USP can trade upon expiration and a profit is still acquired. Selling puts gives you a cushion not experienced when buying a stock outright.

For example, let's say you buy 100 shares of BABA stock for $90 a share. You just dished out $9,000 on this trade. In one month, if Alibaba is still hovering around $90, you have made nothing. If it drops to $88, you lost $200. Conversely, had you sold a put option on this same stock at say a $85 strike price, you would collect income whether it rises, stays flat, and even falls slightly in price.

The reason this occurs is because you get paid for *time decay* when you are the option seller. So each day that goes by (including weekends and holidays), that put option is decaying further in price. And considering you're the option *seller*, a decay in price equates to money in your pocket!

When selling puts, the smallest amount of time until expiration should be one month, with no limit on how far out you want to go. This means, along with monthly puts, LEAP put options can be quite lucrative. This is especially true when highly regarded companies are lagging behind the market, such as after corrections or crashes.

The amount a put option pays out is directly correlated to the IMV of the option. For this reason highly volatile stocks, such as those in the tech sector, tend to pay out more than less volatile stocks. Let's go over a real world examples of selling puts.

Selling Puts: WFC Example

In March of 2020, the whole market went into a tailspin and most stocks fell heavily in the process. It was unclear what would happen in the world, or how much Covid-19 would impact the stock market. However, just a few months later, the market was back to its previous highs and the world was getting back to normal. Nevertheless, in the fall of 2020, many bank and energy stocks were still trading at 52 week lows, having not yet recovered.

Based on the improving economy and the fact other sectors of the market had already recovered, you could safely assume sometime in the near future, bank and energy stocks would rise from the ashes, or at the very least not decline much more.

On Monday October 19th, 2020, Wells Fargo (WFC) closed the day at $22.54. Looking at LEAP options, you would have noticed an ATM $22.50/p, expiring on January 21st, 2022 (1.25 years away), was trading for $3.80. Doing the math ($380/$2250), you could have earned a 16.89% return on this option (held to expiration), which equates to a yearly return of 13.51%. Considering the S&P 500 averages around 9% a year, 13.51% is a very beneficial payout!

And again, we're selling a put option here. This means Wells Fargo could stay flat, move higher, or even go down slightly over this time period, and we would still make a hefty return on this trade.

When the option expired on January 21st, 2022, WFC closed at $55.00. Would a greater profit have been made if we bought WFC outright? Yes, but we don't have the luxury of knowing the future in the moment! What we did know however, is we essentially had a guaranteed 16.89% return so-as-long as Wells Fargo stayed above $22.50.

What was beneficial about this strategy is we were trading a reputable, blue-chip company. We weren't selling a put on an IPO or tech startup, but instead a well-known company that was struggling somewhat after a crash, but would more than likely move higher over a one year period. But even if it didn't move higher and stayed at $22.54, we still would have made our profit of 16.89%.

Let's now go over another put option trade, except with a shorter time period on a more volatile stock.

Selling Puts: BABA Example
It's the middle of August and you notice Alibaba (BABA) has been experiencing increased IMV. You like BABA and would not mind owning it long term if assigned a put option.

You pull up the options chain to find a put option that will expire in one month (September). BABA currently trades for $90.03, and you decide to sell a cash-secured $85/p for **$2.76**. This means your broker sets aside $8,500 worth of your funds until the option expires.

Scenario A: BABA Increases Slightly (Sell $85/p)
In one month, BABA closes at **$92.00**. Because the USP expired above your strike price, you get back your full collateral of $8,500, while also retaining $276 in premium. You make $276 on this trade, a 3.25% profit in one month ($276/$8,500).

Scenario B: BABA Declines Slightly *(Sell $85/p)*

In one month, on the day of expiration, BABA is trading for **$84.00**. You close out your put option for $1.02 before the market closes to prevent it from being exercised into your account. You make $174 on this trade, a 2.05% return ($174/$8,500).

Scenario C: BABA Falls Deep *(Sell $85/p)*

On the third Friday of September, around 3:00pm, BABA is trading for **$80.00**. You decide you will let the option be exercised into your account, as you like the stock and believe it will rally in the near future. On Monday, you own 100 shares of BABA, at average share price of $85. You currently sit with a loss on this stock of $224.

As you can tell by this example, selling put options can be quite beneficial from a risk/reward standpoint. In scenarios A & B, you made money whether the stock increased, stayed flat, or even traded slightly below your strike price!

And then in scenario C, had you bought 100 shares of BABA outright at $90.03, come September you would have been down over $1000. But by selling an OTM $85/p, you essentially get the stock at a discount, while also getting to keep the premium from the put option you sold, thus reducing your loss to just $224.

This is why selling puts on stocks you wouldn't mind owning can be beneficial. Because even if the stock expires below your strike, you then get a stock which you expect to improve in the future at a large discount.

There are times when certain put options have exorbitant IMV (*e.g. tech stocks*), where selling a put 50% below the USP still pays out very well. If you decide to sell puts in these scenarios, just be aware of the earnings date of said company. While earnings generally produce minor movements, they sometimes can cause huge swings in the USP (*e.g. 20%+*). In other words, you may want to avoid trading put options on very speculative stocks when the put option expires *after* their earnings announcement.

Covered-Calls

Where would this list be without including covered-calls? With a covered-call, you're essentially renting out your stock each month to someone who thinks the price will expire higher than it currently trades.

A common premise advocated by investment "educators" is the idea you can sell OTM covered-calls forever on the stocks you own, and they will never be exercised because they will never reach the price you sell them for. Put another way, you can get "free money" every month by selling far OTM covered-calls.

For example, let's take a look at the ETF QQQ, which currently trades for around $306. Scanning very far OTM call options one month out, you'll find a $350/c sells for $0.23. This means if you sell one of these call options while owning 100 shares of QQQ, so long as the ETF doesn't expire above $350 in one month, you make $23.

Most months QQQ will never rise this high, allowing you to collect the premium on the call option you sell. Years could go by where this same scenario plays itself out, and you continue to collect "free" money every month.

Eventually however, do to normal market forces, QQQ will expire higher than the call option you sold. And when it does, your shares will be exercised, causing you to "miss out" on the gains past your strike price. Not only this, due to your shares being exercised, you will now owe taxes to the government from all the profits you made on QQQ.

I performed a personal study where I backtested selling OTM covered-call options on SPY for 10 years (linkpony.com/covered). Ultimately, no matter how close or far you went with your OTM covered-call option each month, you would have made more money simply holding SPY *without* selling covered-calls.

Why am I telling you all this? The reason is to dismiss the claims that some online "educators" make in regards to *long-term* covered-call use. Covered-calls can be a great strategy to use, but I would argue only for stocks in which you *don't* plan to hold long-term. Stocks in which you plan on selling at some point in the future at a specified target price. Let's go over some examples.

Covered-Calls: UAL Example
It is August, and you currently own 100 shares of United Airlines (UAL) at an average cost per share of **$36.42**. Pulling up a chart of United Airlines, you notice it hit a high around $50 about 4 months ago, so you decide you want to make $50 your target selling price.

You take a look at the options chain for UAL, and find a OTM $50/c LEAP which sells for $1.07. This option expires in January, which is 5 months away. You decide to implement the trade and now own a covered-call.

On the third Friday of January, UAL closes at **$56.75**. Your 100 shares of United Airlines are exercised away from you because UAL closed above the $50 strike of the call option you sold.

You make $1358 ($50.00-$36.42) in stock appreciation, as well as $107 from selling the call — a total profit of $1,465.

Covered-Calls: OXY Example

It is August, and you currently own 100 shares of Occidental Petroleum (OXY) at an average cost per share of **$73.24**. You don't think there's much upside potential left in this stock and want to get out at $80.

You pull up the option chain for OXY and find an OTM $80/c expiring next month (September) with a premium of $2.34. You sell the option and now own a covered-call on your 100 shares of OXY.

On Friday, in the third week of September, OXY closes at **$78.22**. You make $498 from an increase in the USP, as well as $234 from the call premium — a total profit of $732.

Since OXY expired below your $80 strike, you get to continue to hold the stock and can sell another covered-call which will expire next month, continuing this process indefinitely until OXY expires above $80.

◆ ◆ ◆

Notice in these examples that you owned a stock that you *were going* to sell at a certain price. These are not long-term stocks in your portfolio, but instead short-term trades in which you have a set target on the USP.

With these types of short-term swing trades, covered-calls become a beneficial strategy to employ as they allow you to collect extra money while your shares get to their target price. And if the USP goes *above* your strike price by expiration, it doesn't matter because you were going to sell the stock at that price anyway.

On the other hand, if the stock stays flat or does not reach your target price, you get to keep the premium received from the covered-call, and can repeat the process every month until the stock expires above your strike.

In summary, you are selling covered-calls on a stock that you own, but which you plan on selling at a higher price in the future. You are not selling covered-calls on stocks/ETFs that you are holding indefinitely because, in most cases, you will not end up making as much as just holding the stock by itself in the long-run.

Deep ITM Leaps

Generally speaking, trying to double or triple your returns in the stock market requires taking out a margin loan with your broker. These loans come with heavy interest fees and can be quite risky in the event of a recession. There are many horror stories on the internet of people taking out loans to buy stocks or options and then losing it all in the process.

But what if there was a way to double the amount of money you are investing, without paying any interest *and* without any increased risk... would you be interested?

This will come as a shock to many but there is, and it comes by way of deep ITM call options. Using this strategy, you are able to essentially double your buying power *without* increasing risk or taking out any type of loan.

If you remember from *Chapter 1*, delta is the amount a call option moves in price relative to its USP. For example, if a call option has a delta of 0.98, this means it moves 98 cents for every dollar the USP moves — almost a dollar for dollar match.

And when you pull up an option chain, you will come to find the deeper ITM you move, the higher the delta becomes. Knowing this, let's go over an example of how we can use this information to increase our buying power with options.

Stock XYZ is trading for $100. Pulling up the option chain you discover the following information for an ITM LEAP option:

- ❖ Strike Price: $50
- ❖ Premium: $50.45
- ❖ Delta: 0.95
- ❖ Expiration: 6 months away

In summary, buying this option right now would cost you $5,045. Conversely, if you were to buy 100 shares of stock XYZ right now, it would cost you $10,000.

And since this call option has a delta of 0.95, this means for every $1 increase in the stock price, your call option will increase by $0.95. This signifies an almost dollar for dollar match with the USP, allowing you to buy 100 shares of this stock for half the cost!

And that is the general gist of this tactic: buying deep ITM call options with far-term expiration dates, which end up costing much less than buying 100 shares of stock outright. Here are the rules you want to follow when using this strategy:

Rule #1: *Delta > 0.90*

This is to make sure your call option moves as close as possible to a dollar-for-dollar match with the USP.

Rule #2: *Strike Price is Half of the USP*

Half of the USP is usually the sweet spot for this strategy. Strike prices closer to ATM will cost less, but will have a lower delta. Strike prices deeper ITM will have a higher delta, but will cost more.

Rule #3: *At Least 120 Days to Expiration*

You are the option buyer in this scenario, so time decay is something that must be taken into account. The further to expiration, the less time decay will be a factor on the option premium. So while 120 days until expiration would be the bare minimum, the further you go out the better.

An additional benefit of this strategy is the way the USP affects the delta. As the USP moves *up* in value, so does the delta on your call option. Meaning the call option inches closer to a true dollar-for-dollar match with the USP.

Furthermore, when the USP moves *down* in value, the delta decreases. So the amount you lose on your call option actually becomes *less*. With this all in mind, let's go over a real world example using this strategy.

Deep ITM LEAP: AAPL Example

It's January 1st and the new year has just arrived. Your grandma just deposited $8,000 into your bank account after she discovered you spent all your money trying to date an OnlyFans model on your iPhone (who still hasn't called you back). You've always had a love for Apple products and want to invest in the company long-term.

When you open your brokerage account, you discover that Apple (AAPL) is trading for **$155.65**. You'd like to buy 100 shares of this stock but don't currently have enough money. Then you remember you can buy an ITM call option, which allows you own 100 shares of the stock at half the cost.

You look at Apple's option chain for ITM LEAP call options that expire in two years. You find a call option with an $80 strike price (about half of the current $155.65 price), with a delta of .9877 and a premium of $76.98. You pull the trigger and put in an order to buy the option, costing you $7,698.

Now let's go over a couple of future scenarios that could come from this trade.

Scenario A: AAPL Increases *(Buy $80/c LEAP)*

Two years go by, and AAPL is now trading for **$230**. Your call option expires ITM, and you are provided 100 shares of Apple in your account at an average cost of $80 per share.

Considering the $7,698 you spent on the option, as well as the current USP, you make a total profit of **$7,302**.

Had you bought 100 shares of Apple outright two years ago (which would have tied up an additional $7,867 in capital), you would have made *just $133* more on this trade.

Scenario B: AAPL Decreases *(Buy $80/c LEAP)*

Two years go by and AAPL is now trading for **$140**. Your call option expires ITM, and you are provided 100 shares of Apple in your account at an average cost per share of $80.

Considering the $7,698 you spent on the option and the current USP, you lost $1,698 on this trade.

Had you instead bought 100 shares of Apple outright two years ago, you would have lost about $130 less than with your call option. But... and this is a big but... an additional $7,867 in capital would have been tied up over this 2 year period.

Notice in these two examples, whether you bought AAPL outright ($15,565) or bought the ITM call option ($7,698), you made and lost essentially the same amount of money. Additionally, think about all the extra capital tied up when buying the stock outright. You could be using this money to invest in other stocks, or even buying two ITM call options, doubling the amount of profit you make on this trade.

It really is a have your cake and eat it too with this strategy. There are only a few minor disadvantages which you should be aware of:

1) No Dividend

You do not collect a dividend while you own the call option. However, a small dividend (*e.g. 2%*) does not come close to the amount you save in capital using this strategy.

2) Illiquidity

Deep ITM call options tend to be rather illiquid. Meaning it is hard to get in/out of them without losing some money on the bid/ask spread. Therefore, while you can sell the option at any time, you really should plan on holding the option until the expiration date when you initially enter the trade. Put simply, this trade is meant for stocks which you plan to hold *long-term*.

Bear-Call Credit Spreads

Selling calls and shorting stocks are a great way to bet on sinking companies, but they carry large risks. Back in my hay days, I lost more than I care to admit shorting "sure" losers. Watching the stock shoot up in price not only cost me money, but accounted for many sleepless nights where I awoke just to check how a short was performing in my brokerage account.

Credit spreads allow you to partake in the dark arts, all while limiting the risk to a predetermined amount. And while certain credit spreads (*e.g. bull-put*) can be used to bet on appreciating stocks, I prefer to use them as a shorting mechanism.

For these reasons, credit spreads are a great way to engage in educated stock market gambling, whereas these same gambles would be rather risky using naked calls or shorting stocks outright.

We'll now go over a real world example of credit spreads in action.

Bear-Call Credit Spread: AAP Example

Advanced Auto Parts (AAP) is currently trading for $110.83, hitting a new a 52-week low this week. Remembering what you learned from Jesse Livermore in Reminiscences of a Stock Operator, you recall the quote, "Go long when stocks reach a new high. Sell short when they reach a new low."

With this outlook, you have a few ways to profit from a decline in AAP:

❖ *You can short the stock, but with short interest fees and the unlimited risk potential, do you want to?*

❖ *You could sell a naked call, but what if the stock rises in value from some type of black swan event?*

Weighing the rewards and risks, you decide to implement a *bear-call credit spread*. You look for strikes one month away, and decide to trade the following:

► Sell $111/c for $4.15
► Buy $115/c for $2.23

You have now established your bear-call credit spread with a strike spread of $4.00. The most you can make is the difference in premiums, $197. The most you can lose is $203. The initial margin taken by your broker to implement the trade is the difference in strikes, $400.

Scenario A: AAP Decreases *(Sell $111/c, Buy $115c)*

A month comes and goes. AAP has not decreased as much as you thought, hovering around **$110.20**, well below your $111/c. Both your calls expire worthless and you make the max allowable profit on this trade.

▷ Result: +$197

Scenario B: AAP Increases *(Sell $111/c, Buy $115c)*

Two weeks after you establish your spread, investors in China put in a bid to buy Advanced Auto Parts, taking the company private. The stock shoots up in price to **$150.45**. You decide to just let your options expire and lose the maximum amount you can on this trade.

▷ Result: -$203

I kept this example short, as you're already familiar with credit spreads from *Chapter 3*. But I now want to go over how this same situation would have fared using other short selling techniques.

Had we instead **shorted** 100 shares of stock, we would have made almost nothing in scenario number one (or may have even lost money due to shorting fees). In scenario number two, having 100 shares short would have put us in a tough situation trying to decide when to cover our shorts as the stock rose, losing thousands in the process.

Had we used a **naked call**, we would have made quite a bit more ($218) in scenario number one. But this small gain wouldn't really matter to us if we were in scenario number two. Here, just like when we shorted 100 shares of stock, we would have been checking our brokerage account everyday deciding if and when to get out of the trade. Our losses would have continued to pile up, along with the uncertainty of how high the stock price could go.

As you can tell from these alternatives, there may be a little bit more profit to be made, but that comes with an undefined risk if you're on the wrong side of the trade. And if you've ever shorted a stock before, you know the gut-wrenching feeling when the stock shoots up in price and you *are* on the wrong side of the trade. You are then stuck with the difficult decision of whether to continue to let your losses mount in the hopes the stock will fall back down, or to get out of the trade then and there at a considerable loss.

The credit-spread alleviates all this, as you have a defined max-loss and max-gain that is set in stone. Along with this, time is on your side considering you are the "sell" side of the trade. Meaning on nights, weekends, and holidays, that option is losing value and putting money in your pockets, even if it doesn't move one penny in price.

For these reasons, credit spreads are a better way to bet on losing stocks versus other short selling alternatives.

The 20% Solution

A Long-Term Investment Strategy that Averages 20.13% Per Year

Discover a long-term investment strategy that earns an average of *20.13% per year!* This strategy can be implemented in any brokerage account, requiring only 4 trades per year. Putting *just* $10,000 into this strategy 34 years ago would have turned into $3.6 million today. Find out more at the link below.

<u>linkpony.com/20</u>

Final Thoughts

This book contains a lot of information and a number of different option strategies to try... but Rome wasn't built in a day. Considering this, I highly suggest using a practice account before putting your hard earned money into options. Practice the strategies I mentioned in this book, as well as others you may find online, and wait until you feel comfortable with them before trading with actual capital.

You have to practice anything to become proficient. Don't make the same mistakes so many others have and lose your hard-earned money before you understand how options work. Learn, practice, grasp the concepts, and *then* start trading with your real money.

The broker Webull offers a "paper money" account which allows you to practice options strategies before trying them out with real money. Use this link to get up to 12 free stocks just for opening a free practice account: linkpony.com/webull.

Also, feel free to check out my Amazon author page to find more informative books I have written regarding stock and option strategies at: amazon.com/author/timmorris.

If you need a refresher for any of the terms mentioned in this book, a glossary can be found on the next pages. Good luck in your financial journey!

Glossary

$40/p - signifies that the strike price of the option is $40 and you are trading a put (p) option

$40/c - signifies that the strike price of the option is $40 and you are trading a call (c) option

Assigned – when, upon an ITM expiration, 100 shares of stock (for each option contract) is provided to an option trader on the assigning side of the agreement; the price of the shares correlate with the strike price of the option; call option buyers and put option sellers receive *regular* shares; call option sellers and put option buyers receive *short* shares

ATM – at the money; the closet strike price to the underlying stock price

Breakeven Point – the point where you will lose $0 on an options trade

BTC – buy to cover; when you are an option seller and are closing your position

e.g. – example given

Exercised – the ability to end an option contract early and assign yourself 100 shares of stock, for each contract traded, at the specified strike price; typically referred to as "exercising" your option

Expiration Date – day when option contract expires; occurs in after-market hours on day of expiration

HV – historical volatility; the volatility of a stock throughout its history

IMV – implied volatility; the volatility of a stock in the present moment

ITM – in the money; upon expiration an ITM option contract will be exercised

IV – intrinsic value; the value of the strike price subtracted from the USP

LEAP – long-term equity anticipation option; the longest-term options you can trade which typically expire on the third Friday in January; can be one, two, or three years into the future

Margin - the amount that must be initially provided to the broker when conducting certain trades; all or some of the margin is provided back when the trade is closed or expires; also called *collateral*

OTM – out of the money; upon expiration an OTM option contract will expire worthless

Premium – the amount you pay when you buy an option or the amount you receive when you sell an option; the price of the option

Strike Price (/s) – price which correlates with whether your option is ITM, ATM, or OTM upon expiration; also correlates with cost of stock shares upon assignment

Time Value (TV) – the value given to an option which relates to IMV and is calculated from subtracting the IV from your option

USP – underlying stock price

Printed in Great Britain
by Amazon

42420609R00071